We're Already Home

TERRY JORDAN, LORNA TURESKI AND ARNIE HAYASHI

Wild Sage Press

For performance rights please contact:
alreadyhomeplay@gmail.com

cover art: *these were no islands he was passing* by Terry Jordan
book/cover design and typography: LM Publication Services Ltd.
printed and bound in Canada:
Houghton Boston – Saskatoon, Saskatchewan

paper: Enviro 100 (text) and
        Productolith Points (cover)
fonts: Schmutz (headings) and Stone Sans (text)

Library and Archives Canada Cataloguing in Publication

Jordan, Terry, author
    We're already home / Terry Jordan, Lorna Tureski,
Arnie Hayashi.

A play.
ISBN 978-0-9881229-7-0 (pbk.)

    I. Tureski, Lorna, 1962-, author II. Hayashi, Arnie, 1953-,
author III. Title.

PS8569.O727W47 2014   C812'.54   C2014-905114-X

Publishing made possible with the support of Creative Saskatchewan

creative
SASKATCHEWAN

Wild Sage Press
www.wildsagepress.biz

We're Already Home was started somewhat in earnest a year ago this past winter with the interests and working imaginations of a group of wonderful, intelligent people belonging to the Vernon Interfaith Bridging Project. I was hired as dramaturge to shepherd the participants through the often-challenging process of creating a play, and wound up working with two brilliant new playwrights. Lorna, Arnie, what a pleasure. Our aim, all along, was to connect ideas with characters to create story in a meaningful way. The purpose of the Interfaith Bridging Project is also to connect: people, their different communities and faiths with imagination, understanding and tolerance. All of us — writers, actors, the directors — hope the efforts we've made will help in this regard, if even a little.

From the beginning, for their support, sage advice and enthusiasm, the writers would like to thank Debora Messer, Harpal Dillon, Mary McLean, Sara Gabriel and Suman Dillon. Nola Dibski, never wavering, never doubting. Shon Thomas for his humour, intelligence and guidance.

The writers relied heavily on consultation with, and the patient generosity of, Sana Mohammed and Mohammad William Creelman of The Vernon Mosque and Islamic Centre, Mollie Bono and Jack Spotted Eagle of the Okanagan Nation and the many from the Vernon Christian Community who unselfishly gave both time and insight to the project. Our gratitude.

Finally, Opening Night was ecstatic, unforgettable. Selling out a 250 seat theatre was more than our hopes allowed. We owe a great debt to everyone who worked so hard to make the run a success. The cast was luminous bringing the play off the page, giving it life. Barb, Christian, Dash, Debra, Martin, Mike, Narinder and Sydney: a thousand thanks to all of you. Let's do it again.

Terry Jordan

Cast of Characters

ROY: early 50's

RUTH: late 40's

JACOB: 17

ALI: 40's; a slight hybrid-London accent

AISHA: 40's; a faint English school accent

SILA: 17

VIOLET: Manifests as any age and in any form
               she likes. A Senklip/Coyote trickster spirit
               figure of the Okanagan Syilx people.

An earlier version of this play was first performed
March 14, 2014 at the Powerhouse Theatre, Vernon, BC
with the following cast:

ROY   Michael More

RUTH   Barb Fitzpatrick

JACOB   Christian Armstrong

ALI   Dash Taheri

AISHA   Narinder Bal

SILA   Sydney Cochrane

VIOLET   Debra Bob

NARRATOR   Martin Niedballa

The play was directed by Shon Thomas and Terry Jordan.

Lighting/sound was by Randy Jones.

Setting

Extreme upstage right is a box used as a promontory for VIOLET. Painted black and even when lit, it should not stand out; she will almost seem to be floating on it, whether standing, sitting or lying down.

Even though the families live across the street from one another, on stage the two houses are side by side with a wall (short in length but not in height) separating them. The two interiors are almost mirror images with the exception of slightly different furniture choices, religious symbols and same-sized paintings on the back walls. Both houses have a short flight of three or four steps off their wings leading to a landing suggesting second floor rooms facing the street.

ROY's lazy boy chair and a small table beside it fill the Gibbons landing. In front of the chair is a window frame topped by a triangle suggesting an upstairs dormer. The Ahmed landing is used as SILA's room. Each house has an outside door that opens out to the wings. The respective walls facing the audience each contain a picture window looking out on the street and are invisible.

Directly in front of the dividing wall are a table and chairs used equally by the two families as if they are in their kitchen, RUTH's BullsEye Workplace, etc.

Downstage front is used as the street, walking path, etc.

ACT I

The following three short scenes are separate but the second and third scenes start before the scene previous to it is finished. The lights do not go down on the first and second scene until the third scene is finished. A character from one scene might turn slightly as if hearing something of interest in another scene.

Scene 1

Interior of the Gibbons home. ROY is in his chair reading, almost falling asleep. He takes off his glasses, leans back and sings softly.

ROY: *(to the tune of an old Spiritual)* Oh, Jesus Lord he walked on the water/Said follow me to heaven in the name of my Father/Save us all like lambs from the slaughter...

The singing fades into sleep.

Scene 2

Interior of the Ahmed home. ALI picks up a cardboard box from the table which has arrived in the mail. He opens the box and takes out a seemingly ordinary empty jar, handling it with care.

ALI holds the jar up at eye level, smiles.

ALI: Ah, another one. I am blessed.

ALI reads the accompanying note, bows his thanks and fixes a white label to the jar.

Scene 3

Lights up on VIOLET who has overseen both these scenes without comment. When VIOLET points the cane she is carrying at ALI, he almost drops the jar but catches and saves it. VIOLET's smile suggests she has something to do with the incident, either causing it to fall, saving it, or both.

Scene 4

The lighting changes to simulate sunrise. VIOLET stands centre stage, eyes closed, arms outstretched. She slowly turns around once, soaking up the sun.

VIOLET: I'm not a morning person. In fact, some people say I'm not a *person* at all, but I do love waking up in the Okanagan Valley! I've been away a long time, tmXUI'A/Xw! I could be blind but I would always be able to tell when my weary body has landed here! Mmm, the smell of lake water drifting on the morning breeze, pine sap warming up in the sun...

VIOLET opens her eyes and gazes all around, studying the landscape.

Look at how you've changed! Why, I knew you when the glaciers were as tall as these hills, again when the ice crawled away and the lakes were born. The balsams took root on these beautiful, sage soaked hills. Oh, I've missed you tmXUI'A/Xw!

VIOLET rubs her body. The rubbing changes to scratching. She gives herself a good scratch all over, exuding ecstasy.

The sun on my fur feels so good! But it wakes up the fleas, too!

VIOLET stops in mid-scratch to look at the audience. She addresses them directly, her hands on her hips.

What are you looking at? Have you never seen a coyote before?

VIOLET continues to stare down the audience, then slowly turns to look behind her, continuing to turn while craning her neck to look at her behind.

Darn! Where did I leave my tail this time? My memory plays jokes on me after ten thousand years.

VIOLET looks like a dog slowly chasing its tail. She stops and wiggles her fingers, feels her face, rubs her behind thoughtfully.

I remember now. *This* story calls for a *woman* who can look like many people, or be invisible. And those are just a couple of the tricks I use. Ask the creator, I didn't just come here for a holiday; I go where I'm needed, where the creator sends me. Though there was that time I snuck off to … well, never mind. Sometimes I trick myself. I'm just glad I found my tail *that* time because living without a tail is like swimming down the Fraser River through Hell's Gate without a rudder.

VIOLET turns around once more with arms outstretched, then stops and cocks her head to study something.

Wait a minute! This is not the ponderosa pine I know and love. This is a newcomer!

VIOLET picks a conker up from the ground, holds it up, examining it with a jeweler's eye. She sniffs, then licks it tentatively and yelps.

Horse chestnut!

She looks up, way up.

Looks like you've been here a while, too, eh? Spreading your conkers and leaves outside people's houses like this is your right? *(pause)* Hmmm, where have I heard that story before?

VIOLET examines the horse chestnut in her hand.

Prickly little suckers on the outside, but not so bad when you peel away the outer layer. *(confidentially)* Like some people I know.

VIOLET gives the audience a sly look, and stretches a mighty stretch.

Time to soak up some sun and find out what's happening in the neighbourhood. Maybe I can turn this into a working holiday...

Scene 5

Gibbons home. ROY stands at the upstairs window, looking out. JACOB sits at the kitchen table listening to his iPod as he eats his breakfast toast.

Roy shakes his head, calls.

ROY: What a mess. Branches blown this way, leaves scattered that. Damn tree uses the neighourhood as its private bathroom!

JACOB takes out his earbuds.

JACOB: Dad! What's the matter? What are you so grumpy for?

ROY: There's the proof right there that that tree's gotta come down — there're tree weeds growing in our yard! Dozens of its dirty little children where they don't belong!

JACOB: Why don't you go clean them up?

ROY turns.

ROY: It's not exactly the easiest thing for me, running stairs like a pup.

JACOB: You're the one who climbs up there. Why don't you stay down here where...

ROY: Why don't you take out your headphones now and then?

JACOB: Dad.

ROY: Maybe that's something you can do.

JACOB: Dad...

ROY: Clean them up, I mean.

JACOB: Dad, they're earbuds.

ROY: What?

JACOB: Earbuds, not headphones.

ROY: And if beggars wore headphones, horses would... listen...

JACOB: What?

ROY: Hang on. Listen. Remember we talked about renting a cherry picker and taking that big sucker down. Start at the top, fire up the saw...

JACOB: There are people living there again. You can't just go around cutting people's trees down like some crazy vigilante logger. Besides, Sila loves that tree.

ROY: Sila? Who's that, and what kind of name...?

JACOB: She's the girl who lives there. Her family's Muslim.

ROY: How do you know her? And how do you know she *loves* that tree? And that she's...

JACOB: She's in some of my classes at school. And I,
         like ... *talk* to her ...

ROY: Well, that tree could hurt someone, even her.
         We could've bucked that wood up.

JACOB: We don't have a fireplace.

ROY: Or sold it.

JACOB: It's not ours.

ROY: Or given it away.

JACOB: Helloooo ... *it's not ours* ...

ROY: Jesus on a tractor, Mister Smartypants! Why
         don't you just give it a rest?

JACOB: Watch your language, Dad.

ROY: Watch *your* language ... *and* your attitude!

JACOB: God.

ROY: What did I just tell you, Jacob?

         *JACOB shakes his head, but doesn't say
         anything else.*

ROY: Those chestnuts are rickety when they get old.

JACOB: Cranky, too.

         *ROY stares down the stairs as if daring
         JACOB to continue. JACOB rises, takes his
         last bite of toast, drinks his milk.*

JACOB: I gotta get to school.

ROY: Can you pour me some coffee before you go?
         Where's your mother?

JACOB: It's Wednesday. She's on mornings.

ROY: Aren't her mornings Tuesdays and Thursdays?

JACOB: She had it changed. She told us.

ROY: Where is her work schedule? How am I supposed to keep track when she keeps taking every lazy-body's shifts so they can go to Hamilton or Mexico or God-knows-where, for crying out loud.

JACOB: Hamilton?

ROY: People die or have babies or get married, and not necessarily in that order, in Hamilton same as any other place, don't they? Darlene, works cash, *she* went. I don't know why, but she did! Okay?

JACOB: Okay...

ROY turns awkwardly from the window and begins a slow journey down the stairs toward RUTH's work schedule on the wall. Half way there he stops, rubs one of his legs, obviously in pain.

ROY: Where's the calendar?

JACOB: Where it always is.

ROY's impatience grows into rage.

ROY: I thought she and I were supposed to take the car in for an oil change and rent some new movies together this morning! Otherwise, I'm trapped here like some damned rat!

JACOB: Dad!

When ROY finally reaches the calendar he feels around on top of his head and realizes he's left his reading glasses by the window. He looks impotently back where he has come from.

ROY: DAMN IT!

JACOB: Take it easy, Dad!

ROY points up the stairs.

ROY: Glasses. *(pause)* Glasses! Can you get them for me?

> *The last part of ROY's sentence is cut off by JACOB's cell phone ringing.*

JACOB: Hey, Tristan! What's up?

> *JACOB walks off-stage talking into his phone as ROY is left standing.*

ROY: Jacob? *(pause)* Glasses? *(pause)* My coffee? *(calls)* JACOB!

Scene 6

> *JACOB is outside the house on the phone with his friend Tristan.*

JACOB: Yeah, you heard right, but I didn't get the part. I knew it was a long shot... well, I've never done any acting before, have I? *(pause)* Yeah, I know, but I was just trying to get Sila Ahmed to notice me. *(pause)* It's called a hijab. *(mispronounced as high-jab)* She's a Muslim. *(pause)* Don't you dare! If you post anything on Facebook, I'll kick your... *(pause)* You better not, you'll screw up any chance I have to get to know her. *(pause)* What do you know? All you ever think about are the Canucks and *Call of Duty*. *(pause)* Are you going to the party at the lake this weekend? *(pause)* Ok, I'll see you there.

Scene 7

> *Lights up and immediately the sound of street traffic. RUTH and AISHA have recognized one another and are stopped together on the sidewalk. RUTH has a purse slung over her shoulder. AISHA is carrying a small bag of groceries.*

AISHA: Hello. You're…

RUTH: Yes. Across the street. Hello, I'm Ruth.

AISHA: Yes, I remember. You live in the blue house.

RUTH: Green, actually.

AISHA: Oh, forgive me. That again. I'm colour blind, you see.

> *RUTH laughs.*

AISHA: No, really I am. I still don't know why. I have been since I was a little girl. It's embarrassing at times.

RUTH: Oh…well, that's a good way to be these days! My son Jacob brought home…I think he goes to the same school as your daughter…

AISHA: Sila.

RUTH: Yes. He brought home a pamphlet this last week asking that we all try to be blind to colour. You know what I mean. It's good.

AISHA: Yes, it's good. I think it's a good school.

RUTH: How are you liking your new home?

AISHA: Oh, it's still in a tip with the move. I've hardly slept, there's so much to do. Outside, too.

RUTH: You've got that old chestnut tree in your yard.

AISHA: Yes.

RUTH: We've been in our house since before Jacob was born, I've watched that tree grow. It's like it's wearing a Hallowe'en costume now, it's gotten so big. I don't know what they were feeding it. Leaves all over the block.

AISHA: It's really the only mature tree in the neighbourhood. We love trees.

RUTH: Did you know that there are thousands of trillions of leaves that drop all over the world each year, I can't even imagine that! *(pause)* Not that all the leaves come from your tree, mind, but Roy, my husband, he doesn't get around like he used to. He has a hard time raking leaves. He thinks that old tree is going to come down one of these windy fall days and you might be safer to cut it down.

AISHA: Oh... we couldn't do that...

RUTH: They sometimes get rotten on the inside and all it takes is that one little push... and you've got all those little seedlings starting up in everyone's yard.

AISHA: But, that tree is one of the reasons we bought the house. Mohammed (Praise be upon Him) has said that "Never does a believer plant a tree, but that he earns the reward of charity from what is eaten from it."

RUTH: Oh no, you can't eat those nuts! You'll start to whinny. It's a *horse* chestnut tree. *(giggles)* Uh... I'm going to embarrass myself, but you'll have to remind me again of your name.

AISHA: Well, we all have to watch what we eat... By the way, thank you for the food you brought over for us. That was very nice. *(pause)* I'm Aisha.

RUTH: Oh, thanks for saying. I'm terrible with names sometimes. I didn't want to ask again, but then how would I know? Did you like it? Not your name, your name's beautiful, but did you like the food?

AISHA: Well...

RUTH: It's an Italian chicken dish I found on TV. We had friends over and they loved it so I thought I'd make it again.

AISHA: Oh.

RUTH: But, it occurred to me that maybe you don't eat meat. You're not vegetarian, are you?

AISHA: No…

RUTH: Good. *(pause)* Oh, sorry. I didn't mean it that way. I don't mind what people eat…

AISHA: *(quickly)* We've been meaning to have you over. We've been busy with sorting out the house and all. Like I said.

RUTH: I was just going to the little store here. *(points)* I need some gum for work.

AISHA: I'm just coming from there. I know the owners. Their parents and my parents were from the same town.

RUTH: Oh, really! Where?

AISHA: In Iran.

RUTH: Is that where you were born?

AISHA: Yes, but my parents moved us to England in the '80s after the war began. That's where I met my husband Ali. And now we're here.

RUTH: Just like that.

AISHA: Well, not exactly. *(laughs)* I don't want to bore you.

RUTH: Oh, don't worry about that.

AISHA: Well, the house is a bit mysterious.

RUTH: Is it?

AISHA: Did you know the person who lived there before us?

RUTH: She was elderly. Her son moved her to a Home, I think.

AISHA: Chinese, I think, yes?

RUTH: Yes. Mrs. Wu.

AISHA: Because when we moved in there were bags and bags in the garage waiting to be thrown out. All manner of things, everything tied up in brown paper wrapping and string with Oriental writing on them. Photographs, figurines, sewing notions, boxes of cookies, even an old-style camera, and best of all, for Ali, dozens of jars. Empty…well, filled with air.

RUTH: Air?

AISHA: Yes. Old jars, some with script on them. My husband collects jars.

RUTH: Antique ones? Valuable jars?

AISHA: No, just jars. Well, not *just jars*, actually. Jars filled with air.

RUTH: Oh.

AISHA: From different places in the world. With air captured inside from a certain city, or event or moment. He likes to imagine…

RUTH: Like photographs.

AISHA: Yes, exactly! It's kind of silly. But lovely, too.

RUTH: Yes, that is lovely.

AISHA: The elderly lady's son, Mrs. Wu's son, didn't seem to want her things. It was terribly private, but like Christmas, too. Opening all those packages. I shouldn't be telling you this, but he was just going to throw them out.

RUTH: Do you celebrate Christmas in Iran?

AISHA: Christians do.

RUTH: There are Christians there?

AISHA: There are Christians everywhere. But,
          we're Muslim. We have our own festivals,
          celebrations. Right now it is Ramadan and
          we are fasting.

          *AISHA lifts the bag of groceries she is
          carrying.*

          We won't eat this until after dark.

RUTH: You do have rules what you can eat, what you
          can't. Roy said you might.

AISHA: It's called *halal*.

RUTH: Oh. I noticed that word on the store window.
          (pause) So...you didn't eat my Italian chicken
          after all?

AISHA: Oh dear. No...I'm sorry, Ruth. I should have
          told you right away.

RUTH: You couldn't have eaten it even if you wanted
          to, could you?

AISHA: We did want to. It smelled delicious. But no,
          we couldn't. You were so generous and I
          didn't want to offend you.

RUTH: You couldn't offend me with a stick. *(smiles)*
          Like my mother always said, "Acting like
          everybody doesn't make you anybody. You've
          got to be yourself and give everyone that
          same freedom." She celebrated the things
          that made people different. Your husband
          collects jars, mine was in the seminary. He
          studied to deliver the word of God and wound
          up delivering the mail.

Scene 8

Lights come up with ROY in his chair. VIOLET is laboriously walking up the stairs toward him, one hand on her aching back, using a cane. ROY has finished drinking coffee, has put down his newspaper. He is staring out the window. He picks up the home phone from the table beside him and punches in a number. As he does, VIOLET abandons her farcical mime and hurries forward, all health and vigour, and leans her cane against his chair.

ROY: Roy Gibbons. G-I-B-B...yes, that's right. 279 Tobermory Heights. What? In Scotland. What the...? Yeah, you're funny. Listen, I told you, I don't know the license plate number. I can't see it from here. *(pause)* No, I can't go see. Not today. *(pause)* No, I can't. *(pause)* It's not that I won't...Pardon? No, there's no one down there. There's nothing to be afraid of. It's just an eye-sore. Yes, it's abandoned. The bylaw gives someone a week to park their vehicle, that's all. I checked. *(pause)* What do you mean the Bylaw Division? What are you saying? That there has to be a bomb in it before you'll come out? *(quickly)* Okay, sorry, I didn't mean that. Everything's so blasted touchy these days. *(pause)* Yes, it's an abandoned vehicle. In front of my neighbour's house. Yes, on the street. *Not* in the yard. *(pause)* I don't know if it's theirs. Could be, I don't think so. It makes me nervous. It could be anything, including dangerous for all I know. Yes. And it's ugly. *(pause)* What do you mean, what do I mean it's ugly? It's a rusted, patchy, badly painted-by-hand, son of a Volkswagen wreck with mismatched tires and cracked windows. *(pause)* It does have some bumper stickers with bright colours. I can't read 'em from here either, but they look ugly, too.

ROY stands with the help of the cane.

How do I know it's a Volkswagen if I can't read? *(voice rising)* Who said I can't read? I never said I couldn't read! What?

ROY puts the phone down.

God help me.

ROY picks up phone again.

I can read as well as the next person, just not from this distance and my binoculars are downstairs. *(pause)* I'm not shouting. *(pause)* Yes, I realize that. Yes. No, I don't have a choice. Take my word for it. Do you understand? NOT TODAY. Some days I can, some I can't. Some days it's cane, some I'm able. Today … not so much. *(pause)* Yes, that's exactly what I mean! *(pause)* Okay. I'll watch for you.

ROY shakes his head, hangs up the phone.

Scene 9

Interior of the lunchroom at BullsEye. RUTH is in her work uniform sitting at the downstage table, eating her lunch out of a brown paper bag. VIOLET is sitting across from RUTH.

RUTH: Why is it that lunch break flies by so fast when the rest of the day crawls by so slowly? Half an hour just isn't enough time to eat properly. My egg salad sandwich just doesn't want to go down.

RUTH rubs her sternum.

You don't have any Tums in your purse,
do you?

> *VIOLET opens her ridiculously large purse,
> hauls out all manner of objects: a wig she
> puts on and a hand mirror she primps in
> front of, etc. During all of this RUTH stares
> straight ahead, glumly snapping the lid of
> her Tupperware sandwich container off and
> on, off and on.*

VIOLET: Um, checking.

RUTH: It's Annie, isn't it? Give me a few more
times seeing your face, a couple more shifts
together and I'll have your name down, I'm
a face kind of person, need that visual to
connect the name, you know?

VIOLET: Mhmm.

> *VIOLET applies bright red lipstick as she
> looks in the hand mirror.*

Sorry hun, no Tums.

> *She pulls a banana from the purse.*

Banana?

RUTH: What? No, that's okay, thanks for looking.

> *VIOLET kisses herself in the mirror and
> preens.*

VIOLET: You're welcome!

RUTH: Phew, I haven't had heartburn like this since I
was pregnant and my stomach was squeezed
half way up to my throat. Do you have kids,
Annie? Annie, Annie, Annie. There, I've said it
three times, that should make it stick.

VIOLET: Yes, I have children.

RUTH: Then you know what I'm talking about, heartburn, constipation, peeing every ten minutes. I have one, a son, graduating next spring. How many do you have?

> *VIOLET has been eying a box of donuts that was left on the table for the staff. She is a bit startled when Ruth asks her the question, but can't take her attention away from the donuts.*

VIOLET: Mmmm, donuts! Twelve little sugar coated…children!

RUTH: Twelve! Are you Mormon? Catholic? What church do you go to?

VIOLET: The Church of…

RUTH: No offense, it's just not that often you hear of anyone having so many kids these days, not even Catholics!

VIOLET: Our Lady of Fur-till-i-tee.

RUTH: That's a new one to me. But then I was never very good with the saints' names. Is that the one they just built on Pleasant Valley Road? We don't go anymore, with Roy having MS and all.

> *RUTH coughs, covers her mouth with one hand.*

You don't have any Halls in there, do you?

VIOLET: I do have Life Savers!

> *VIOLET rummages through her purse and triumphantly comes up with a partial roll of Life Savers. She offers them to RUTH, who takes one and pops it into her mouth with delight.*

RUTH: Oh, lucky me, I got a cherry flavoured one, they're the best. But we better keep our distance. I'd hate to pass my germs to you.

RUTH fiddles with the Tupperware container.

Annie, do you ever think about what's going to happen when all your kids are grown up and gone? Jacob, that's our son, he's practically an adult now, so busy with grade twelve, says he's going to McGill, says, no way is he going to UBCO and live at his parents' house.

And Roy, well, some days he might as well be gone, he already is in a way, the Roy I fell in love with.

Back in the day, I went to youth group just because he was the leader, not that I wasn't a Christian, but I really thought about Roy, probably more than I thought about Jesus, God help me, but you should have seen Roy then! I can see him in my mind's eye right now, wearing Levis and a white t-shirt, very Bruce Springsteen. He looked so sharp it was like he was outlined in black pen. Now, I see him crunching through a bowl of Fiber One cereal every morning, a little river of milk running down his chin, and I think I need my reading glasses, you know, to see Roy better but they don't help. Roy has just gone all blurry and I don't know how to bring him back into focus.

RUTH coughs suddenly and begins choking on the Life Saver. VIOLET jumps up to slap her on the back, and after much drama, performs the Heimlich Maneuver. The Life Saver pops out of RUTH's mouth.

Annie! *(gasping)* Oh, I remembered your name! Annie! You saved my life! I couldn't breathe! Couldn't get any air at all.

VIOLET: Air's kinda important. Probably the first time someone's life had to be saved from a Life Saver, though. Well...

RUTH stands, hands at her throat, she's all aflutter after her near-death experience.

RUTH: I've never thought about air before! It's just there, we breathe it and so what? But we're toast without it! No wonder a person might collect air! What a brilliant idea! If I had a jar I'd save some of this air, right here, right now! Air from the day you saved me, Annie!

VIOLET pulls a jar from her bag, hands it to RUTH.

RUTH: Annie, you are amazing!

RUTH scoops air into the jar, clamps the lid on as though she has just captured a creature.

I'll make a label when I get home. "Air from the day I almost died." No, "Near-death air!" That's better isn't it?

VIOLET slings her purse over her shoulder and walks offstage, leaving RUTH in rapt adoration of both her jar and VIOLET.

Scene 10

JACOB and SILA are walking home from school. JACOB is several feet behind SILA. SILA stops, but does not look behind her.

SILA: Jacob Gibbons, quit following me.

JACOB takes a few more steps toward SILA before stopping.

JACOB: I'm not following you! I mean, I *am* following you, Sila Ahmed, because you are not the only one who lives on Tobermory and doesn't drive a car. So yes, I *am* following you, because...

SILA: Because sadly, we both belong to the car-less group known as The Walkers...

JACOB: And sadly, that is not likely going to change before graduation.

JACOB moves a few feet closer to SILA.

SILA: I've got my "L" — I just need to get in some driving time. *(pause)* Okay, Jacob, that's far enough.

JACOB: You have your learners? You're allowed to drive? What do you mean, that's far enough?

SILA: Of course I have my learners. I'd have my "N" too if my parents weren't so afraid to get in a car with me behind the wheel. I mean you can't come any closer.

JACOB: I wasn't sure if you were allowed to drive.

SILA: Jacob...

JACOB: You can call me Jay.

SILA: Oh, like Beyoncé's husband, only Jay G. instead of Jay Z.? Anyway, this isn't Saudi Arabia where a woman can't have a driver's license. And you can't come any closer because I am a Muslim girl and it's not proper for me to be alone with a boy, especially not a boy called Jay G.

JACOB: Seriously?

SILA: Seriously.

JACOB: They're not allowed to drive there?

SILA: Not women.

JACOB: And you can't walk home with me?

SILA: No I can't, it's not allowed, either.

JACOB: Sorry about the Saudi Arabia thing... I suck at geography.

SILA: *(giggling)* Religion, too! It's okay. There aren't a lot of Muslim girls at our school, so how would you know?

JACOB: Well, there's always Google. Your hijab *(says high-jab)* seemed kinda weird at first too, but...

SILA: It's pronounced "hijab." But...?

JACOB: Oh, sorry. *But,* I'm used to it now. Besides it looks good on you. I mean you have lots of nice ones. They even match the rest of your clothes.

SILA: *(suddenly a little shy)* You've noticed that my hijabs match my clothes?

JACOB: Well, sure, I saw you at the tryouts for the play, and then you sit just a few seats in front of me in chemistry...

SILA: Hey, what happened with the auditions? I haven't seen you since.

JACOB: Oh, yeah... it turns out I'm no actor.

SILA: I didn't know you were even interested in the theatre. You aren't in drama class with Mr. Thomas, are you?

JACOB: No, I uh... I thought it would be a good way to meet some... new people.

SILA: How did that work out?

JACOB: Well, I'm meeting you now.

SILA: True…umm, well, I'd better go. I have to help prepare food for tonight and I'm late.

JACOB takes off his backpack, rummages inside and pulls out two granola bars.

JACOB: Here. It'll tide you over until supper.

He tosses the granola bar to her and she catches it easily in one hand.

Nice catch!

SILA: I played second base on the softball team at my school in Ontario.

SILA tosses the granola bar back to JACOB.

Thanks for the offer, but I can't accept.

JACOB: But it's the sweet *and* salty kind. They're the best.

SILA: It may be halal, but even then, I can't. It's Ramadan.

JACOB: Halal? Ramadan?

SILA: Halal is that which is permitted by our law, or food that is prepared in a special way. Ramadan is a month of fasting and prayer for Muslims. We're in the middle of it, right now.

JACOB: Hey, can you text me the spelling of those words?

JACOB scribbles on a piece of paper and crumples it up like a softball, then tosses it to SILA.

If you text me then I'll have your number. Maybe we can go out sometime?

SILA looks at the ball of paper, uncertain how to respond.

SILA: Well, my parents, they're…

JACOB: Muslim?

SILA: Exactly!

JACOB: Don't worry, I don't want to excite your
           parents! See you this afternoon? Maybe we
           can walk home together again. I can stay a
           respectable 10 feet behind you.

SILA: Oh, I won't be at school this afternoon, I'm
           going on a girls' class trip. I hate riding on
           buses, and then they're going to make us
           climb those big log towers, team building
           exercises… I'm terrified of heights!

JACOB: Hey…

           JACOB takes off the necklace he's wearing.

           My mom gave this to me, it's a St. Christopher
           medal. To protect you while you're traveling.
           Why don't you take it — it'll bring you home
           safely.

SILA: Thank you, but…

JACOB: No, I want you to have it. I'd feel terrible if
           you didn't take it and your bus went over a
           cliff, or the log tower collapsed…

SILA: Not helping!

           *They both laugh. JACOB holds the necklace
           out at arm's length. SILA hesitates for a long
           moment, then reaches for it, taking a step
           toward JACOB.*

SILA: I shouldn't be taking this. I shouldn't even be
           talking to you.

           *Turning it over in her hand SILA sees the
           initials inscribed on the back.*

           It says J. G.

JACOB: Yeah, my mom had it inscribed. Do you need a hand putting it on?

SILA: No! *(pause)* I mean, that's okay, this is enough for one day. *(pause)* Thanks, Jacob.

JACOB: You're welcome. Okay, I'm passing you now…

> *JACOB passes SILA, careful to keep his distance. He goes offstage.*

> *SILA slips the necklace into the side pocket of her backpack, takes out her cell phone, opens the crumpled paper JACOB gave her and enters his name and texts the words to him.*

SILA: Jay-Gee… H-A-L-A-L. R-A-M-A-D-A-N.

Scene 11

> *AISHA and SILA are sitting at the table preparing food for Iftar, the sunset meal during Ramadan.*

AISHA: I didn't know you only had a half day at school today.

SILA: Mom, you never listen, I told you on Monday.

AISHA: Monday! That may as well have been a lifetime ago! Well, it's nice to have a girls' lunch once in a while with my daughter even if we won't eat.

SILA: Mom, I have to get back to school, I have leadership training this afternoon.

AISHA: Leadership training? What is this?

SILA: Dad signed the permission form last week. He said it was okay, in fact better. than okay, a great opportunity, he said.

AISHA: I'm sure it is. Is it at the school?

SILA: No, we're taking a bus to this outdoor place near Salmon Arm.

AISHA: The bus! You get so queasy on the bus! Did you take any Gravol?

SILA: No, Mom, I haven't. I'm not seven years old anymore!

AISHA: Well as I recall when someone was sixteen years old and went on last year's field trip, someone took Gravol…

> SILA fiddles with her backpack, surreptitiously checking on the St. Christopher medal.

SILA: This time will be different. I'm more grown up, more…

> SILA glances at the St. Christopher in her hand. AISHA reaches into the cupboard and takes down a box of Gravol.

AISHA: Here, take this with you, just in case the optimism doesn't quite do the trick.

> AISHA tries to tuck the box into SILA's backpack but SILA pushes her away, afraid she will discover the St. Christopher.

Sila Ahmed, what has gotten into you?

SILA: Mom! It's just… I'm not a kid anymore, okay?

AISHA: Of course you are not a kid anymore, you're a beautiful young lady! *(suddenly slightly suspicious)* Say, I saw you on the sidewalk with the Gibbons boy. You didn't drive home in that truck of his, tell me you didn't!

SILA: That wasn't a truck parked outside, it was a van, Mom. And Jay doesn't have a truck or a van. He doesn't even drive yet. We walked.

(*trying to change the subject*) What did you do this morning, Mom?

AISHA: Oh, it's "Jay" now is it? How do you know so much about this boy, and what were you doing walking with him?

SILA: Jacob lives across the street; I can't forbid him to walk to his own home. Look at me, hijab on, blouse down to my wrists...it's all good!

AISHA: Yes, the hijab, the modesty is good, but there's so much more when it comes to being "all good"! I know wearing the hijab isn't easy in such a small town, but we've talked about this before; the hijab is only one small part of appropriate conduct for a young woman. Appropriate conduct begins in the heart!

SILA: Don't worry Mom, I'm not going to shame us! I have to go now!

> *SILA walks to the door, slinging her backpack over her shoulder. The doorbell rings, startling them both.*

AISHA: Are you expecting someone, Sila?

SILA: Like who? Jacob? No, I'm not! Are you?

AISHA: I hardly know anybody in this town yet, much less anyone who would come by without calling first...wait, maybe it's Ruth Gibbons.

SILA: Jacob's mom? Why would she be coming over?

AISHA: Because she is my friend...she is becoming my friend! Check and see if it's her.

> *SILA peeks through the peephole in the front door and looks startled.*

SILA: I think it's for me, Mom.

AISHA: Oh, it's not Ruth? Oh well, invite your friend in for a moment. I'd like to meet her.

The doorbell rings again, then a polite rapping on the door. AISHA peeks out the peephole.

AISHA: It can't be for you, it's some boy. Probably selling chocolates for a school fundraiser.

SILA: Mom, it's a boy from school, from my drama class. I'll just go see what he wants, okay?

SILA begins to open the door.

AISHA: Sila, what are you doing? Stop it! Just ignore him and he'll go away.

SILA: Mom, I'm covered. It's all good, like I said.

SILA gestures to her hijab and blouse.

AISHA: You're covered? I don't care if you're wrapped in a blanket, it's not proper for him to come over without your father home.

SILA: He doesn't know. And I won't know what he wants if I don't go out there and find out!

AISHA: No one's going out or coming in. He'll get the hint.

The doorbell rings again.

Well, he *is* persistent.

SILA slumps to the floor with her back against the wall.

SILA: This is embarrassing. He knows we're in here and he'll think we're weird for not answering the door.

AISHA: Sila, sweetheart, how many Muslim girls are there at your school wearing a hijab? We are not *weird*, but we are different.

SILA: But he doesn't know why we're not answering the door. He'll think I don't like him.

AISHA: Like him? What do you mean, like him? How do you like him?

SILA: As a human being, Mom! A classmate!

AISHA: Okay, calm down! Call Allah to mind and ask for the strength to be patient and have faith that this boy...what is his name?

SILA: Matthew...Matt.

AISHA: Matt sounds like an old carpet. Come away from the door, Sila, and have faith that Matthew will understand that our customs are a little different from his.

SILA: A little different? Mom, you have no idea how different we are.

AISHA: As my friend Ruth says, "Acting like everybody doesn't make you anybody. You've got to be yourself and give everyone that same freedom."

SILA: Mrs. Gibbons said that?

AISHA: Well, actually it was her mother.

AISHA helps SILA up.

Matt will get the idea that we're not answering the door and he'll go away. Just put him out of your mind. And I'll try to put chocolate out of mine.

Scene 12

This scene begins as the previous scene is ending. Lights up on ROY at his window as he watches the boy at the Ahmed home. The sound of knocking continues from the darkened previous scene. ROY is obviously upset.

ROY: What are they doing over there?

> *With the help of his cane ROY rises from his chair to get a better look.*

Isn't that the McKinley kid? Why don't they answer? How can they just stand there and ignore him? *(pause, as ROY continues watching)* What's wrong with those people!

Scene 13

> *ROY is asleep in his chair.*

> *ALI is sitting at the table with a few jars on it. He is usually dressed in normal business-office attire, but today he has on a gaudy western shirt, a leather vest, bolo tie and a beat-up ugly cowboy hat a bit large for him. He is wearing his normal shoes. He has a pen in hand and is about to write on a white paper label when AISHA enters. AISHA stops at the sight of him.*

AISHA: Hi Ali. Um...how was work today, dear?

> *ALI is concentrating on the task at hand.*

ALI: Bloody pen.

AISHA: Ali!

ALI: Oh, it was fine, my love. Fine.

AISHA: What are you wearing?

ALI: It was Western Day at work today. Did you forget?

AISHA: No, I saw you leave for work today, dear. But where did you get that hat? And why are you still wearing it?

ALI: From Kent. He's in sales.

AISHA: Did he sell it to you?

ALI: No, I just borrowed it.

AISHA: Oh, praise Allah.

ALI: But he's going to get me some boots. They're red and white. Patriotic.

AISHA: And that waistcoat?

ALI: It's called a vest here.

AISHA: The room's dark. Turn on some lights. You're just like Sila used to be. You'll ruin your eyes. *(pause)* Please take off that hat first, dear, it's ruining *my* eyes!

> *ALI takes off the hat.*

ALI: It's the middle of the day, I shouldn't need electricity to light my way. We have sunshine over our earth to do that. Alhamdulillah.

> *ALI smiles, looks up at his wife.*

I am never in the dark when you are with me, Aisha. You are my light.

> *AISHA kisses ALI on the top of the head. She hands him the package she has just picked up from the post office.*

AISHA: As you are mine. Here, this arrived for you today.

> *ALI opens the package, takes out a jar and letter.*

ALI: Ah, it is from Shaheer.

AISHA: Where did he fill it?

> *ALI reads the letter.*

ALI: Mecca. This spring.

AISHA: He went on pilgrimage again?

ALI: Again, this year.

   ALI hangs his head.

AISHA: You will go someday, dear.

ALI: We are getting further and further away each time we move.

AISHA: Not further from the love of Allah, Allah ta'ala, and the guidance of the Qu'ran, Ali. Not further from the love of your family.

ALI: No, dear. You are right, again. And I am lucky to have you, and this air from...

   ALI speaks as he finishes writing what he had started, and affixes the label on the jar.

   ...Mecca...Yes, at least I have my jars.

   ALI holds up the jar as in praise and sets it gently on its new place on the shelf.

AISHA: You have much more than that.

ALI: *(absently)* Yes dear, you are my light.

AISHA: *(with some gravitas)* You said that. Still, you write in the dark.

ALI: *(still not getting it)* It was not my choice today. I was sitting outside in the sun.

AISHA: Dressed like that?

ALI: I looked up and that man was staring at me.

AISHA: I'm not surprised. Which man?

ALI: The man across the street. The neighbour who is always there, upstairs at his window.

   Lights slightly up on ROY in his chair sleeping.

AISHA: Oh that man. His name is Roy ... Roy Gibbons. I met his wife Ruth this morning by the Persian Market. She's nice. He isn't really staring, is he?

ALI: Mr. Eyes. He's like a painting up there, hanging from the second story, his eyes following you wherever you go. I had to get up and come in here.

AISHA: I'm sure there's an explanation.

ALI: "Mr. Busybody" would be appropriate.

AISHA: Ali! How can you say something like that!

ALI: It's what Mrs. Thompson calls him. She lives around the corner.

ALI hooks his thumb back in her direction.

She was watering her flowers. We talked. He's almost always looking out his window.

AISHA: *(patiently)* Yes, Ali. Ruth mentioned something about her husband having a medical problem of sorts. He doesn't move around well, and so he sits.

ALI: Gibbons, you say?

AISHA: Roy and Ruth Gibbons. There's a son Jacob as well. Sila already knows him. He tried to walk her home from school.

ALI: What! Did you talk to her? Did you make it clear that she is not to be associating with any boys and especially not the son of Mr. Busybody?

AISHA: Ali! Don't be juvenile.

ALI: Isn't Gibbons the name of a breed of monkeys?

AISHA: Ali Ahmed! What a thing to say! You should be ashamed.

ALI: I'm sorry. You're right. *(pause)* Maybe I ought to go visit Roy and introduce myself, explain how Muslim life might be different from theirs.

AISHA: Then, go over and meet the man. Find out these things as a way of being friendly. I will do the same with Sila when Ruth is home. Stop being such a cross-patch. There are reasons for everything. *(pause)* Except maybe those clothes. You're going to change before you go, yes?

ALI: Yes, Aisha.

AISHA: I have to drive Sila from school to the Mosque.

ALI's phone rings as she exits.

ALI: Hello. Yes, speaking. *(pause)* Yes. The police? *(pause)* The van? No, it's not mine. *(pause)* Yes, a half hour will be fine.

Scene 14

Lights up on ALI at home sitting at the kitchen table rapidly dunking a tea bag into a cup. He is still dressed in his cowboy costume. AISHA enters.

AISHA: Oh Ali, I said I'd get that for you.

ALI is obviously upset. He cannot, despite his state, bring himself to finish the phrase "Bloody hell!"

ALI: Bloody … Bloody … !

AISHA: Please, Ali! You must try to calm yourself.

ALI: How can I calm myself when I've just been interrogated! Like a prisoner! You don't know!

AISHA:	I'm sorry, dear, that I wasn't here.
ALI:	Asking questions they had no right to ask. As if we were criminals! Bloody...
AISHA:	Ali, please!
ALI:	Aisha, please! We hardly know our neighbours, and they are all going to think we are thieves and robbers and drug users.
AISHA:	Drug users! What are you talking about?
ALI:	They thought there might have been drugs in the van.
AISHA:	They...
ALI:	The police.
AISHA:	...thought there might have been drugs...
ALI:	In the van. Yes. Or stolen goods or... they had a dog sniffing. Barking. Men were shouting. People out watching. Police in our house.
AISHA:	Did you ask them in? The police, did you invite them inside?
ALI:	Yes. We have nothing to hide.
AISHA:	Did they look through the house?
ALI:	No, my love, they just asked questions.
AISHA:	Did they also ask the neighbours questions?
ALI:	Yes, I believe so.
AISHA:	Are the neighbours thieves and drug users?
ALI:	No, I don't think so.
AISHA:	What was in the van?
ALI:	Nothing.
AISHA:	Nothing?

ALI: It was just left there. Abandoned. Someone's junk.

AISHA: *(giggles)* Did you just say "junk"?

ALI: Yes, I believe I did.

AISHA: You've never used that word before.

ALI: Garbage, then. Trash. *(bad John Wayne accent)* "Get your rubbish offa my street, Pilgrim."

AISHA: *(laughing)* You're watching too much TV.

ALI: *(still John Wayne's voice)* Perhaps the little lady needs to be rescued from these here stampeding cows.

> *ALI hooks his thumbs in his belt and advances on AISHA in a mock cowboy walk. AISHA screams in delight and runs.*

Scene 15

> *The stage is set so that both ROY in his chair at the window and ALI, who is dressed normally again and walking up to the Gibbons home, are lit separately. VIOLET is upstage standing on her promontory with a trumpet in her hands. She is trying to figure the thing out, looking at it this way and that. Blowing tentatively, then with great effort. She makes small sounds, if any at all. She pays no attention to the scene in front of her.*

ROY: Who's that? Wait, is he coming here?

> *ALI looks up to see ROY at his window.*

ALI: There he is. Still there. *(wryly)* Always there. Did he just nod? I wonder, should I wave?

ROY: He's coming to the door! There's no one here to answer it.

> *ROY looks away in confusion just as ALI gives a little embarrassed wave.*

Where's that blasted cane of mine!

> *The doorbell rings.*

ALI: He won't even wave back.

> *ALI rings the doorbell again. He looks up, waits before ringing a third time.*

Hello?

> *ROY turns toward the stairs. He is having trouble with his footing; his legs are betraying him. He makes a guttural sound like a growl and swears at the same time. He barely saves himself from falling.*

ROY: Hang on!

> *ALI takes a few steps back to better see up to the window. He calls, sarcastic and sing-songy at the same time.*

ALI: Hello? I know you're there. I saw you.

ROY: Hold on...wait! I don't have my cane. I'm trying. Sometimes I can't...

> *ROY is struggling to get all of the parts working smoothly, together. As his legs begin to work he takes a step, then stops.*

Stairs.

> *ALI rings the bell once more. And again. ROY is beyond distracted.*

ROY: (calling) I can't...My legs aren't...

*ROY sees his cane a short distance away
and reaches for it. The stretch is too much
and he falls clumsily to the floor near the top
of the stairs. As he is lying there thrashing
in anger and frustration, the doorbell goes
one last time. ROY can no longer bear the
ignominy and shouts.*

SON OF A...!

*As ROY is about to complete the phrase, a
very loud squawk issues forth from VIOLET's
trumpet to cover it. VIOLET, who has been
trying the entire scene to get a decent sound
out of the horn looks up then, surprised,
a little startled, then smiles, pleased with
herself and the instrument.*

*Outside, ALI walks away from the house
shaking his head.*

ALI: What's wrong with these people?

Scene 16

*RUTH is making supper at the table,
chopping vegetables animatedly. JACOB is
helping, sort of, and ROY is sitting there in
a chair a little way off from the others.*

RUTH: You'll never believe who I ran into today!

No one responds.

RUTH: Hello, family? Anybody home?

*JACOB looks up. No reaction from ROY.
RUTH forges ahead, bubbly, animated.*

RUTH: The lovely lady across the street, Mrs. ... oh
darn, I've lost it again!

JACOB: Ahmed?

RUTH: That's it, Mrs. Ahmed!

JACOB: Aisha?

RUTH: That's it! Why Jacob you're a regular
         neighbourhood directory!

ROY looks balefully in JACOB's direction.

RUTH: Well, she really is a sweetheart, though it
         wasn't easy for her to admit that they didn't
         eat the chicken, you know, the Jamie Oliver
         recipe I took over? Not that they didn't want
         to, but they couldn't, because it wasn't,
         hmmm... what is that word...

JACOB: Halal.

ROY frowns, interested.

RUTH: Bingo! Yes, halal. Too bad, really, I think the
         recipe was good! But what could they do?
         So committed to their faith! That takes a lot
         of strength, fortitude. I don't know if I could
         have resisted that chicken...

JACOB: But that's just it, Mom, they have faith.

RUTH: Yes, they do, and that's not all... Mr. Ahmed
         ... there I remembered... has the most
         interesting hobby. Do you know what it is?

ROY: Cultivating that blasted tree in his front yard?

JACOB: *(groans)* You're not still obsessed with the tree!

ROY: Obsessed? I'm concerned! That tree is a
         disaster waiting to happen. Any day now a
         branch could come down and conk...

JACOB: Sila...

ROY: ...conk Sila, the Ahmed girl, right on the
         head!

RUTH: Boys! Enough with the tree! Mr. Ahmed is much more interesting than any old tree. Listen, he collects jars, but not just any jars! Jars filled with air!

JACOB and ROY both turn to look at RUTH.

RUTH: Yes, air! From all over the world, people send him jars, filled with exotic, exciting air! Air from holy places, even air from Mrs. Wu's house!

JACOB: Air from Mrs. Wu's house?

JACOB wrinkles his nose.

What part of Mrs. Wu's house?

ROY: It doesn't get any more exciting than dusty jars filled with air from Mrs. Wu's house...

RUTH: There were jars from China, with Chinese writing on the labels. I think it's a romantic hobby.

ROY: Is that a Muslim thing, collecting jars filled with air?

JACOB: Dad, don't you know anything about Islam? I agree with Mom, it's a cool hobby.

ROY: I believe your mother said it was a romantic hobby. So you think it's romantic, do you?

JACOB: *(suddenly wary)* Maybe it's more quirky than romantic.

ROY: And what's with this sudden interest in all things Muslim? Wouldn't have to do with a certain girl who lives across the street in a quirky, Muslim house, would it?

RUTH: Right, she's in your grade at school, her mom and I were just talking about you two this morning. Such an interesting family. I've never met anyone Muslim before.

JACOB: I'm just getting to know her, as a friend. You don't just go up to the door and invite yourself in!

RUTH: Why not?

ROY: That's exactly what that McKinley kid did today.

JACOB: What? Matt McKinley?

ROY: Yep, he went right up to the door, rang the doorbell and everything.

JACOB: And he went in? He visited Sila at her house? Was her dad home?

ROY: If he wasn't home then, he was later when the police came to ask him about that van.

RUTH: Roy, what van?

JACOB: You mean that old Volkswagen that's been parked on the street? It's gone.

ROY: You bet it's gone. I called the cops and they came out and took care of it, had it towed away once they made sure it wasn't loaded with explosives or anything.

JACOB: Wait. You called the cops and told them it was Sila's dad's van? Are you kidding me?

ROY: I didn't tell them it was anybody's van — just that it was sitting there, an eyesore, possibly, probably dangerous, and they should take care of it! And they did. After they questioned Mr. Ahmed about it, but that wasn't my idea!

JACOB: Are you trying to destroy any chance I have at getting to know Sila?

ROY: Look, I tried to get downstairs to answer the door when Ali came over, but this leg, this damn leg...

RUTH: Wait! Mr. Ahmed came over? To talk about the van?

ROY: Well, he looked pretty steamed so I imagine he found out I was the one who called the cops.

JACOB: And you didn't answer the door? What the hell were you thinking?

ROY: Watch your tongue, young man!

RUTH: We need to go over right now and apologize!

ROY: Apologize! I didn't do anything wrong! In fact, I did something right, got rid of that ugly van!

JACOB: Dad, you're always asking me if I have a girlfriend and when I finally find a girl I'm interested in, you call the cops and tell them her dad is probably a terrorist?

ROY: I did not tell them he is a terrorist!

JACOB: You know, Dad, I can get girls to ignore me, no problem. I don't need your help to do it! What are they going to think of us? And here we are, People of the Book and all!

ROY: You mean Christians.

JACOB: At least you are. I don't know what I am.

ROY: Of course you're Christian. You were baptized for heaven's sake!

JACOB: But what does that mean? How does that make me a Christian? Look at the Ahmeds, they're fasting all day long right now. It's called *Sawm*. And when they do eat, it will be only halal food! Do you have any idea how much devotion, how much dedication that takes?

ROY: Well if it sounds so wonderful why don't you *Sawm* all day and see how you like it.

JACOB: Yeah, well I just might. And if you don't go over there right now and apologize, I'll do it for you!

ROY: Be my guest, Mister Muslimwannabe.

JACOB walks out the door. ROY rises out of his chair to apologize but JACOB is already gone.

RUTH: *(heavy sarcasm)* Good one, Dad.

Scene 17

VIOLET is mischievously raking horse chestnut leaves from the Ahmed yard into the Gibbons yard. She is obviously enjoying doing it as she is whistling and almost dancing as she scoops another rake-full into the pile.

She watches from the dark as two shadowy figures in dark jeans and hoodies walk up to the Ahmeds' door. One fools with the lock for a few moments and they enter.

Scene 18

VIOLET watches the two figures leave the Ahmeds' carrying a television and microwave. When they have gone, she drops the rake onto her pile of leaves, goes to the open door and walks inside. A few seconds later she comes back out. She closes the door, and sneaks off, carrying what is obviously a cardboard box of ALI's jars.

Scene 19

SILA, followed by AISHA then ALI, arrive home. They are talking as SILA unlocks the door.

AISHA: Sila! Did you really bring that popcorn home?

SILA: There was lots left, Mom, it was huge.

ALI: What's huge are the prices they charge!

AISHA: But it tasted like puffed up bird food.

ALI: What, you have something against puffy food?

AISHA: The birds might. Maybe it's food for puffins?

SILA: Hah, Mom. When the birds flew up into the sky at the end of the movie...

ALI: Doves.

SILA: And the kid in the front row, his balloon popped just before. It was as if the *BANG* was what frightened them into the sky. That was cool.

ALI: That *was* cool.

AISHA: They were a bit young to be having a party that late, don't you think?

ALI walks ahead of the other two and flicks on the light.

ALI: What, the birds?

SILA: Oh, Dad, please...

As SILA speaks they all stop and go silent.

AISHA: Ali, what happened here?

ALI walks further into the room.

ALI: Look at this! Look!

AISHA: Ali?

SILA steps close to AISHA.

SILA: Mom?

ALI: The microwave's gone!

AISHA: What's that smell? Is it...?

AISHA puts her arms around SILA.

ALI: I think it's beer. Go outside while I check the
           house. No, don't go outside, there might be
           someone there!

SILA: Mom!

AISHA: *(to ALI)* Ali. *(to SILA)* It's all right, dear.

ALI pats his pockets.

ALI: Aisha, phone the police. Call 911. Sila, do you
           have your phone?

SILA does not respond.

           Sila!

SILA: What, Daddy? Yes, I have my phone.

AISHA: Let me see it, Honey.

SILA: I can do it, Mom.

SILA punches in the number.

           Hello? Yes, our house has been broken
           into... Sila Ahmed... Yes, we're all right...
           284 Tobermory Heights... No, I don't think
           they're here any more...

> *SILA and AISHA put their heads together at
> the phone and turn away from the audience.
> Their talk to the 911 responder is silent from
> then on.*

ALI: Stay there and I'll go see …

> *ALI turns and walks, circling the table then
> back into the living area of the house. The
> painting that was on the back wall is now
> missing.*

ALI: *(calling)* The television's gone. The computer
… the music system …

> *ALI stands facing the audience as he studies
> the wall.*

There's something written on the wall!

> *SILA turns from the phone, calls.*

SILA: What is it, Dad?

> *ALI walks back out to join AISHA and SILA.*

ALI: *(bravely)* Nothing, Sila, darling. They've taken
everything, even stolen my jars! *(pause)* What
would they want with empty jars?

AISHA: What about the painting from back home?

ALI: Gone.

AISHA: Oh, no!

SILA: What did they write?

ALI: Nothing, dear. Stay away from there, Sila.
Promise me.

SILA: Okay, Dad.

> *ALI holds out JACOB's St. Christopher medal
> for his family to see.*

ALI: Look at this. They must have dropped it during the burglary. It's got the initials "J. G." on the back.

SILA and AISHA come forward to look.

SILA: That's Jacob's.

SILA's hand flies to her mouth as she realizes she has made a mistake.

But he wouldn't...

ALI: Jacob who, Sila? Who is this...?

AISHA: Jacob from across the street, Ali.

ALI: The son. I'm going to go talk to him.

SILA: But he would never do something like this...Dad, please.

ALI: How did it get in our house, then?

SILA pauses, looks away then back to her father.

SILA: I don't know.

ALI: I think we've got this almost solved. That family who is so good at phoning the police on us.

AISHA: Ali, wait...

ALI: I think it's time we told the police about them.

SILA: Dad, no!

SILA rushes past her mother out the door.

Scene 20

JACOB is out walking. He is surprised to meet SILA, who is in tears.

JACOB: Sila, is that you?

SILA looks up, confused.

SILA: Jacob?

JACOB: What's the matter? Why are you crying?

> *JACOB goes to hold her but SILA backs away.*

SILA: I knew I shouldn't have…

JACOB: Shouldn't have what?

SILA: I knew it was wrong…

JACOB: Oh Sila. What…?

> *JACOB again steps forward to hold SILA.*
> *She warns him away.*

SILA: Don't. Just don't!

> *JACOB steps back, hands in the air.*

JACOB: All right. All right. *(pause)* Can you just tell me
          what happened?

SILA: Something, something happened.

JACOB: What? Sila, what happened?

SILA: *(sobbing)* Our house… we were robbed.
          My house!

JACOB: What?

> *SILA can only nod.*

My God! Are you okay?

SILA: Yes. But…

JACOB: Your parents? Are they okay?

> *SILA is too upset to speak.*

JACOB: Oh no, Sila, come here.

> *JACOB tries to put his arms around her but*
> *she won't allow it.*

You're shaking!

SILA: I'm so scared! They wrote something on
        the wall!

JACOB: It'll be okay! You're safe! Your parents, are
        they okay?

SILA: No, they're not okay! Dad found your
        St. Christopher medal.

JACOB: Okay…so hey, it got you home from that bus
        ride safely! That's a good thing!

SILA: He thinks…he thinks…

JACOB: What?

SILA: He thinks you broke into our house!

JACOB: *(laughing)* That's ridiculous!

SILA: It fell out of my backpack!

JACOB: You didn't tell your dad I gave it to you?

SILA: No, I…I panicked. I'm sorry! He's calling the
        police!

        She begins to cry again.

JACOB: This is crazy! Sila, you need to tell your
        parents…the police, what happened!

SILA: I know…it's just…I'm sorry.

        SILA hears something off into the distance.

        That's my dad! I've got to go.

        SILA runs off.

JACOB: Sila!

        *JACOB watches her for a moment, then runs
        after her.*

Scene 21

> *The Ahmed home. AISHA is drying a teapot she has just washed.*

Scene 21a *is played simultaneously with Scene 21.*

> *ROY is asleep in his chair in the Gibbons home. The spot on him is very low and rises ever so slowly throughout the scene.*

AISHA: I'll have to wash everything in this house. *(pause)* I think I'm going to be sick.

ALI: Are you all right, dear? Do you need something for your stomach? Would you like to lie down?

AISHA: I need a flood, a fire to cleanse all this at once.

ALI: It's all right, now.

AISHA: It's not all right! Not yet! How could I lie down? They might have been in our room. They could have touched anything. Everything!

ALI: Maybe we should stay in a hotel tonight.

AISHA: Look at this!

> *AISHA turns, arms outstretched.*

We have too many things, Ali. What do we need all this for? *(pause)* Look, we've even got two teapots. Why do we need *two*? Do we drink out of two?

ALI: We need three cups. Two parents, one daughter, three rugs for praying.

AISHA: Do you think they touched our prayer rugs? Oh Ali, have they stolen them, too? Did you check?

ALI:	No, dear. Yes, dear. They are safe. They have not been touched. I checked.
AISHA:	Oh, thank you. Praise be to Allah. *(pause)* There is always something to be thankful for, isn't there? *(pause)* No, we will not be forced out of our home and into a hotel. Who knows who stayed there last. Maybe even the robbers!
ALI:	Aisha?
AISHA:	Yes, Ali.
ALI:	Where's Sila?
AISHA:	She's just outside, isn't she?

ALI opens the door, looks out.

ALI:	Not any more.
AISHA:	She was just there.
ALI:	Call her.
AISHA:	I see her phone on the table.
ALI:	It's dark. The thieves might still be around.

AISHA hurries to ALI, looks out herself.

AISHA:	Do you think so?
ALI:	No...I don't know.

ALI looks out the front window.

AISHA:	She just needs a bit of time, a break, to get away. It's been a shock for all of us. I don't want to be in here, either.

AISHA shivers.

Anyway, the police should be here soon.

ALI:	*Again. (pause)* There's that Gibbons, still looking.

AISHA: Where?

ALI: Where he usually is. Up high in his nest.
           The eagle. That's what I'll call him. I've had
           enough.

           ALI begins to gesture at ROY.

           Get away from there! Mind your own business!

           ALI turns back to AISHA.

           An eagle with a magpie for a son!

AISHA: Ali, stop that. Maybe he saw the robbers?
           Did you think of that?

           *ALI marches to the table, finds a phone book
           and pages through it.*

ALI: I'm sure he did, but would he phone the
           police on his own family? No. *(pause) (loudly)*
           Where is Sila? Maybe he was here, too,
           helping his boy! Did you think of that?

           *ALI punches numbers into the phone. He
           stops at the last one, holds the phone above
           his head and walks to the front window. He
           holds the phone up for ROY to see.*

           (shouts) Are you going to answer if I call you,
           or just sit there staring at us?

AISHA: Ali, please control yourself... This isn't going
           to... He can't hear you.

           ALI turns, shouts up at ROY.

ALI: Answer me!

           ALI punches the SEND button on the phone.

           You sit up there all day watching, maybe you
           can tell me who stole into our home! Maybe
           you can do some good and tell us where our
           Sila is!

Scene 21a (continued)

> *The Gibbons home, with lights up fully now. The phone rings. ROY stirs from his nap.*

RUTH: *(from offstage)* Roy, the phone's ringing. Can you get it, please?

> *ROY fumbles with the phone beside him, knocks a cup off the table beside him.*

ROY: Oh...hell.

> *ROY answers, still half-asleep.*

Hello...What? *(extremely confused)* What? Your daughter?

> *ROY sits up in his chair.*

Who is this?...Who? Is everything all right? What are you saying? No, I don't know. How would I? *(pause)* The police? On Jacob? What are you talking about?

> *ROY calls offstage.*

Ruth!

> *ROY turns back to the phone.*

What did you just say? Spray paint? Yeah, we've got spray paint. What the hell's that got to do with... *(pause)* What did you just say about my son? Did you just call him a thief? Why don't you come out from behind your phone and say that again? *(pause)* Where?

> *ROY bolts up out of his chair, and stands looking down from his window, strong and vibrating with rage, all evidence of his infirmity now gone.*

ROY: I see you! Don't move!

> ROY throws down the phone and begins to leave. As he does, his cane gets tangled up in his legs. He picks it up and slams it into the upholstery of the chair, then throws it aside.

RUTH!

> As RUTH hurries out into the living room in her pajamas and robe, ROY rushes out.

Scene 22

> VIOLET is furiously carrying armloads of the leaves she had raked into the Gibbons yard back into the Ahmed yard. She kicks the leaves in all directions to try to make it appear natural.

> ROY and ALI appear on either side of her, both in a silent and blind rage. AISHA and RUTH follow behind their respective husbands, calling for them to stop. Upstage, lit softly, SILA and JACOB who have been standing together talking, turn to see.

> Just as the two men are about to strike one another, VIOLET steps forward with the rake in her hands and brings it sharply down between the two men, stopping time. ROY and ALI are both frozen in equal masks of anger and intolerance. She walks between them, stops, looks fully at the audience, shakes her head in dismay.

> Lights down on the men. Lights down gradually on JACOB, SILA, AISHA and RUTH. VIOLET wanders off-stage.

END OF ACT ONE

ACT 2

Scene 1

Interior of the Gibbons home. ROY is standing, looking out the living room window.

ROY: *(singing softly to himself)* I float like a butterfly and sting like a bee, because I'm Muhammad, Muhammad Aliiiii…

RUTH enters, watches ROY throw a few air punches, shakes her head in disbelief.

RUTH: Roy Gibbons, how you are still standing?

ROY: Anger, Ruth, *righteous* anger.

RUTH: You didn't come to bed!

ROY: If you know that then you must not have slept, either.

RUTH: How could I sleep after that catastrophe last night? I'm just sick about it!

ROY: Sick about what, exactly? Sick about me protecting our son? Sick about our neighbours accusing him of stealing and vandalism? Who the hell do they think they are?

ROY fakes a punch at a plant.

RUTH: Roy, stop that!

ROY: Stop what? Stop feeling like I'm *alive* for once? Righteous anger, Ruth, it's flowing through my veins and I think it's cured me! I *(punch)* feel *(punch)* great *(punch)*. It might be a miracle!

ROY raises his arms in a victory stance.

Knockout!

RUTH walks to stand in front of ROY.

RUTH:	Oh, that's been God's plan all along, has it? He set up this whole mess with our neighbours so you could get some *righteous anger flowing through your veins*, burning up your incurable disease?
ROY:	Look Ruth, no crutches, not even a cane. I would think you'd be happy for me. For you! I'm whole again!
RUTH:	Roy, it's called remitting/relapsing MS because that's what it does. You might feel good for a while but it won't last!
ROY:	You just can't accept that I'm feeling better.
RUTH:	I can't accept what happened last night!
ROY:	*(sighing)* Okay … maybe I got a little carried away, but …
RUTH:	No buts, Roy! You started it with that phone call to the police about the van. Got us on the wrong foot with the Ahmeds. And what will Aisha think? She was becoming my friend!
ROY:	I didn't sic the police on Ali Ahmed. I didn't know they would think it was his van! Ruth, I really didn't.
RUTH:	It's too late now, Roy. Mr. Ahmed was just doing an eye for an eye, telling the police about Jacob's medal. I just don't understand how it got into the Ahmeds' house in the first place.
ROY:	He's a teenager, Ruth, he doesn't tell us everything he does, heck he hasn't since he was six years old!
	The adrenaline is wearing off a bit. ROY sits down.

WE'RE ALREADY HOME • ACT 2

But I know one thing, our son wouldn't break into a house and he sure wouldn't write filth on anyone's walls. He likes the Ahmed girl. *(pause)* Wait a minute, maybe we're looking at this all wrong … maybe Sila *stole* the necklace …

RUTH: That's enough, Roy Gibbons! No more stirring the pot! All we *know* is that the necklace was in the Ahmeds' house. Even the police don't think it was Jacob, but if he has nothing to hide why isn't he defending himself?

> *ROY throws a half-hearted punch from the chair.*

ROY: That's what I was trying to do last night, defend him! Look, Ruth, something's going on with Jacob, he hasn't been himself lately.

RUTH: None of us have been ourselves lately, and fighting is *not* the example you need to set for Jacob! Matthew 12:31: "Thou shalt love thy neighbour as thyself"! Not, thou shalt fight thy neighbour …

> *ROY reaches out and draws RUTH closer to him.*

ROY: Hmmm, that old Matthew 12:31 quote, huh? So you do remember some of your youth group homework? That was a long time ago, Ruthie.

RUTH: It feels like a whole lifetime has gone by! But it really wasn't that long ago, was it Roy? When we were going to change the world. Make it a better place.

ROY: It all seemed so simple, sitting in the church basement, making plans, memorizing Bible verses. Now I can't even get my neighbour to cut down a tree.

> ROY *starts to throw a jab, which dies. His hand falls to his side.*

Maybe it wasn't the greatest idea ever to...

RUTH: No Roy, it was the worst idea ever!

ROY: I wasn't exactly thinking in the moment, Ruth. My body was just out there... cashing cheques.

RUTH: That your mouth was writing! Keep it shut unless you're talking to your son. You need to find out what's going on with him. And no more floating like bees!

Scene 2

> *The Ahmed home. AISHA and ALI with brooms, rubber gloves and buckets, sponges. They sweep and clean, wipe down the walls as they speak.*

> *Lights are low throughout the scene on SILA in her room sitting in a chair, head bowed, writing in her journal, pondering her predicament, debating what to do about it. From time to time she raises her head, silently blows her nose.*

ALI: Did you talk to Sila?

AISHA: I tried again. She won't come out of her room.

ALI: What's wrong with her?

AISHA: There were strangers in our house last night who wrote terrible things on our wall! I know how she feels. If we don't wash every inch of this house, I'm not sleeping here tonight.

ALI: Yes. Yes. I know, my dear.

AISHA: You've got to be patient with her, Ali. It's upsetting to all of us!

ALI: Yes. I know.

AISHA: I couldn't sleep after the police were here.

ALI: Did something happen with the police that I don't know?

AISHA: No. It's just everything, like I said. *(pause)* I was happy they had a woman constable here. She was very good at her job.

ALI: Did she talk to Sila?

AISHA: Just for a moment. The constable said she could come back if she had to. *(pause)* I noticed they spent quite a bit of time at the Gibbons' afterwards…

ALI: They should have.

AISHA: Maybe.

ALI: What do you mean, maybe?

AISHA stops cleaning, turns to ALI.

AISHA: Oh Ali, not again. Does he seem like that kind of boy? We can't be sure, can we? And until we can… The police were quite certain there was more than one person here.

ALI: Maybe he had some little tattooed friends along with him.

AISHA stares at ALI for some time until he slips her gaze.

AISHA: And Sila says he would not have done such a thing. She knows him better than we do. The Qur'an tells us that we cannot be given a blessing better and greater than patience. I'm worried about our daughter.

ALI: What does the Qur'an say about vengeance?

AISHA: What do *you* say about shame? About raising
           your hand against your neighbour?

ALI: I brought no one shame! I raised my hand *for*
           my family. *Against* those who would steal our
           things.

AISHA: Thank you for protecting us, Ali. I love you for
           that. But did you hear me when I said I was
           worried about Sila. Our *things*—our television,
           our computer—those... *appliances*... are not
           important. A microwave, your jars. They are of
           the earth, not of the spirit which is where we
           should be...

           ALI interrupts. He's not been listening.

ALI: Why would they take *my jars*? Some of them
           were old and maybe antiques, some had gold-
           coloured tops but...

AISHA: They're just metal and glass.

ALI: No.

AISHA: They're just air, Ali.

ALI: No! They're not just air, they're more than
           that! They're history, family, honour to
           Mohammed (Praise be upon Him).

AISHA: Listen to me, please, Ali. They may be more
           than air other days, but today, when your
           family, your daughter needs you, they are
           just air, and glass, and fancy lids! In a few
           days they can go back to being precious and
           we will do whatever we are able to do to get
           them back. But today you are a husband. A
           father. You are Ali Sher Ahmed. Named for a
           lion by your father Shahzad who was named
           for a prince!

ALI: Yes, dear.

AISHA: Maybe the police have already found them. Besides, Shaheer will send another. Your uncles will, too. We can find more. You can start again. You've been good at that in your life, even before me.

ALI: This is true. *(pause)* But what you've said is even more true. And a more precious thing to find. *(pause)* I do love my wife, my daughter.

AISHA: I know you do, dear.

AISHA kisses ALI on the cheek, then turns to go into the living room with her bucket and sponge and rubber gloves. She stops, realizing this is where the graffiti was.

At the same time, SILA rises from her chair. She begins to walk toward her parents.

ALI: Don't worry, I painted over the spot in the living room. It's all right to go in there now.

AISHA: I wondered what you were doing working in the night. I don't mean to say that you don't look after and love your family, my lion.

ALI: You were finally sleeping. I wanted to have it cleaned before morning prayers, and before you or Sila could read what it says.

AISHA: Thank you, Ali. I didn't want Sila to see it. I didn't want to see it either. I don't want to know. *(pause)* Is it very bad, what it said? Was it about us, specifically, or...

ALI: What it said is not important, Aisha, my love. But the answer to it is.

AISHA: What is the answer, Ali?

ALI: That this *is* our home. That we are *already* home.

By this time SILA is standing in the kitchen entrance way. She is about to dissolve into tears.

SILA: Mom?

AISHA: Oh Sila! Hi, dear.

SILA: Mom, can I talk to you?

AISHA: Of course you can, darling. *(pause)* Are you all right?

SILA: No.

SILA holds her arms out to her mother, begging to be held. She begins to sob.

Oh, Mom.

AISHA rushes to her daughter.

Scene 3

The action takes place in both the Ahmed and Gibbons homes simultaneously, though the lights go down on the Ahmeds much more quickly.

In the Ahmed home AISHA and SILA are sitting on SILA's bed together. They are talking, though the audience hears no dialogue. SILA is explaining her mistake. AISHA listens, embraces her daughter. Lights out.

In the Gibbons home, ROY is alone in the house sitting in his chair in the near-dark, thinking, maybe praying. ROY gets up out of his chair and looks down to the Ahmeds'. When he, again, sits he lays his head back and sings the short bit of song from the beginning of the play, a bit louder than before.

ROY: Oh, Jesus Lord he walked on the water/Said
         follow me to heaven in the name of my Father/
         Save us all like lambs from the slaughter...

         This time he does not sleep.

Scene 4

         Muslim call to prayer is playing softly in
         the background. Spotlight on SILA, who is
         performing ablutions in her bedroom, slowly,
         carefully, with water from a basin. Another
         spotlight is on AISHA, who is doing the same
         in the living room. A third spotlight comes
         up on VIOLET, who is sitting fist under chin,
         watching.

         VIOLET wistfully addresses the audience.

VIOLET: I remember being seventeen like it was
         yesterday. Well, maybe like it was yesterday
         plus a few thousand years.

         VIOLET winks.

Give or take.

         AISHA and SILA raise their arms. Their
         movements are not exactly synchronized,
         but it becomes apparent that they are
         following the same set of ritual movements.

You know, science is showing us that the
decision-making part of the brain, the frontal
lobe, doesn't completely mature until we are
in our twenties. We've learned so much about
the brain! We've come so far!

         AISHA and SILA say, "Bismillah" silently. They
         wash their hands in the water from the basin.

But still the longest road is from here...

         VIOLET touches her head.

...to here.

VIOLET touches her heart.

The head to the heart. The good, red road.

AISHA and SILA rinse their mouths and noses.

I've gotten into a lot of trouble travelling that road. Sometimes I don't even want to look at the map, I just want to hop into a fast car and hit the highway.

AISHA and SILA wash their faces.

I like fast cars, Mustangs and Chargers. Though once in the '60s I had a VW van that I liked a lot. Drove it out here this time around. Parked it there in the street.

VIOLET winks to no one in particular.

Couldn't pass a logging truck going uphill though. That was before they built the Coquihalla. Remember those days?

AISHA and SILA wash their arms.

I remember when there were no roads at all. When fossil fuel slumbered below ground.

AISHA and SILA wash their heads and ears. Finally their feet.

But in that fast car, hell-bent to get some-where, eventually you run out of gas and you don't even know where you are.

Their ablutions finished, SILA and AISHA are ready to say their prayers. VIOLET stands up, brushes herself off, brings a bundle of sage from one pocket, a braid of sweetgrass from the other. They all stand ready to begin their prayers.

But nobody gets anywhere without travelling that road from the head to the heart, the good red road.

> *VIOLET raises her arms and closes her eyes. A traditional Okanagan chant is heard. SILA and AISHA pray silently while VIOLET turns to the four directions. She prays out loud, calling on the directions, the ancestors, etc. The light goes down on VIOLET and we see AISHA kneeling on her prayer rug in the living room. SILA enters the room, stops when she sees her mom. After a moment AISHA carefully rolls up the rug, turns and sees SILA.*

SILA: I'm sorry Mom...

AISHA: That's okay, Sila. I needed a little more time to pray. It's when I feel most safe, when my mind it totally focused on Allah...when I can put aside the world.

SILA: No, I mean I'm sorry, I'm so sorry about everything. If I could take it back, I would. I've never seen Dad like this before. I'm worried about him.

AISHA: He's worried about you. Your father has tried very hard to find a place for us that is safe and just and...beautiful. He feels that he has failed.

SILA: That's what he said to me, too. But I'm the one who failed.

AISHA: No. We make mistakes. We learn.

SILA: That's Dad's line.

AISHA: It's a good line.

SILA: It's just that things...life...can be so confusing! It's not as simple as reading labels on...

AISHA: Jars.

SILA: ... on granola bars and fighting the Great
           North American Personal Jihad of finding halal
           foods to eat!

AISHA: You are practically an adult, Sila, and you must
           carefully weigh the decisions you make.

SILA: Sometimes I feel like an adult, but sometimes I
           just want to be seven years old again.

> *The light comes up again on VIOLET who
> slowly lowers her arms as though she has
> just finished praying. With her eyes closed,
> she stands with one hand on her forehead,
> one hand on her heart.*
>
> *AISHA steps forward and places her hand on
> SILA's forehead.*

AISHA: Here, I know you are seventeen and a young
           woman ... but here ...

> *AISHA places her hand over her own heart.*

           ... here, you are still my little girl, your father's
           little girl.

> *AISHA pulls SILA into her arms and holds her.*

           Your father needs time to process it. He will be
           fine. You, we, will be fine.

Scene 5

> *The phone rings in the Gibbons home as
> RUTH is entering the house. She is carrying
> groceries. The answering machine picks up.*

VOICE: Hello Roy, it's Marnie down at the auction
           house. You asked me to let you know if we
           ran across any jars, right? What are you doing,
           making pickles? *(laughs)* Sure enough, a

whole box of 'em showed up. Some of them are different, a bit old, just like you wanted. Anyway, come on down and you can bid on them. Okay? See you then. Bye.

Scene 6

The exterior of the Gibbons home, just outside the front door. ALI is standing on the doorstep. He raises his hand to ring the doorbell, then drops it. He repeats this several times, and just as he is going to leave, the door suddenly opens, startling him.

RUTH: Mr. Ahmed! I thought I heard something out here!

ALI: Mrs. Gibbons!

RUTH: Come in, come in!

ALI: Thank-you, Mrs. Gibbons, but I'll just stand here for now.

RUTH: Oh please, it's Ruth.

ALI: Mrs. Gibbons, Ruth...

ROY, sitting in his chair upstairs, calls down.

ROY: Ruth, who is it?

RUTH: It's our *neighbour*, Mr. Ahmed.

ROY: Oh, it is, is it? I'll be right down.

ROY stands and begins his journey down the stairs. He is not quite as nimble as he was after the fight. The audience watches him labour as RUTH and ALI talk outside.

ALI: Call me Ali, please.

RUTH: Thank you. I will.

Awkward silence.

The weather is...

ALI: ...the weather.

RUTH: Warm...

ALI: For this time...

RUTH: ...of year. *(pause)* Mr. Ahmed, Roy's behavior was completely out of line, I told him...

ALI wipes his forehead and neck with a cloth handkerchief, holds up a hand to stop RUTH.

ALI: Mrs. Gibbons, please.

RUTH: He's acting like Muhammad Ali! Oh I'm sorry, that's probably blasphemous!

ALI: No, that's quite all right. I think the Prophet (Peace be upon Him) understands a little bit about boxing.

ROY steps into the doorway, obviously winded with the effort of navigating the stairs.

ROY: Ali, if you're looking for round two, I won't even be able to make it out of my corner.

ALI: Please, I'm here to right a terrible wrong. I accused your son of a crime, but it has come to my attention that I was mistaken.

ROY: Oh?

ALI: Sila, my daughter, my one and precious daughter...

RUTH: She's lovely, really she is...

ALI: Sila has confessed—informed us—that your son...

RUTH: *(helpfully)* Jacob...

ROY: Shhh, Ruth, let the man speak.

ALI: Jacob...

ROY gestures impatiently.

ROY: Yes, our son, Jacob…

RUTH: Roy!

ALI: Your son, Jacob, gave the St. Christopher necklace to our daughter…

RUTH: *(unable to help herself)* Sila…

ALI: Yes, to Sila, as a gift, a thoughtful gift to assuage her fear of heights and vomiting and it pains me to realize that I accused your son of the horrible crimes that were committed at our home.

ROY: Yes?

ALI: And… I'm sorry. Really, terribly sorry for wrongly accusing Jacob. Please accept my apology.

ROY: *(finding a bit of his Muhammad Ali fire again)* I don't know that we can just erase what happened, phoning the cops for crying out loud…

RUTH: Roy! You phoned the police, too.

ALI: It's okay, Mrs. Gibbons. Mr. Gibbons, Roy. I myself have harboured some ill-will toward you since you called the police about the vehicle that was parked on our street. I know the boiling anger that comes from being falsely accused.

ROY: I never accused you…

ALI holds up his hand.

ALI: I correct myself. I know the boiling anger that rises in the belly from *believing* one is falsely accused. All I ask is that you think about accepting my apology.

ROY: Well...

RUTH: We can do better than that, Roy! Of course we accept your apology, and hopefully you accept ours. Right, Roy?

ROY mumbles his agreement.

You and your family must come over for dinner. Nothing mends fences like breaking bread together. Halal bread, of course.

ALI: Oh no, really, that's not necessary!

ROY: Oh geez, Ruth, he's right, that's not necessary.

RUTH: There's very little in life that is necessary, but many things that are good. I think this is one of those things that is necessary *and* good!

ALI: I think Sila is still a little too embarrassed to visit. And it is Ramadan. We do not eat until the sun is down.

RUTH: Then I'll make dinner for you some night. Maybe tomorrow?

RUTH stares defiantly at ROY.

Roy will deliver it to you. Maybe we'll come over together. Excuse me, I'm going to check on a few recipes...

RUTH goes back inside, leaving ROY and ALI uncomfortably alone on the doorstep. Lights go down slowly.

Scene 7

RUTH and JACOB are in the kitchen hiding from ROY. VIOLET is behind them nodding rhythmically, moving a bit, barely dancing, her hands cupped over her ears as if she's wearing headphones. She's not paying attention to the Gibbons.

RUTH: How may people would be interested in a box of old jars? There might be a couple of pretty ones in there, but I mean no one's going to know there's air inside going back as far as the Bible.

JACOB: Hardly that, Mom. *(pause as he thinks)* What if someone's opened them? What if they've let all the air out?

> *VIOLET stops dancing, interested now. She takes her hands away from her ears, listens.*

JACOB: Do I still bid on them?

RUTH: *(pause)* I suppose. *(shrugs)* They'd still be his jars.

JACOB: Who would know? *(pause)* It's just something you can't see, right? Would he know? *(pause)* But we would know, wouldn't we?

RUTH: Yes, we would. *(pause)* I don't know if it would matter if the original air was inside the jars or not. But it's an issue of faith. Mr. Ahmed *believes* in that air. It's symbolic. He believes it's in the jars. If it was an... What am I trying to say?

JACOB: If it was an illusion...?

RUTH: If it was an illusion to everyone else, he would still believe. It's like this old silver locket of Grandma's I wear.

> *RUTH lifts the locket up from its chain around her neck.*

Picture of you inside and it's fused shut over the years, but I still believe you're in there and you still bring me joy and give me strength. I don't need to see it. Because I believe.

> *Both RUTH and JACOB pause.*

So, yes, go and bid on those jars. Let's make a
neighbour happy, give him back some faith.

JACOB: He'll be surprised.

RUTH: Your father doesn't know about it, either. I
erased the message. We'll surprise him, too.

JACOB: How much should I bid?

RUTH: As much as it takes, I guess.

Scene 8

ROY sits in his chair talking on the phone.

ROY: Is it too late? *(pause)* Tonight? *(pause)* I
thought you were going to tell me. *(pause)*
Oh? On the machine. No, I didn't. Bloody
Jacob, he never remembers to pass messages
along. *(pause)* Can I put in a bid over the
phone? I can't make it down. *(pause)* I don't
know. How high can it go for a box of old
jars? *(pause)* Twenty bucks? *(pause)* No,
Marnie, I don't want to lose them. *(pause)*
They're just bloody jars, not jewels. *(pause)*
Okay, okay. Yes... Okay. Make it a... are you
sure? *(pause)* Okay, make it a hundred, then.
(pause) Sure, why not? Why not a thousand?
(pause) No, I'm kidding! I'm kidding. A
hundred will be fine. Just a hundred and they
better not reach even close to that. I'm not
that crazy.

Scene 9

The doorbell rings in the Gibbons home.
RUTH goes to the door, opens it. It's AISHA.

RUTH: Aisha! Come in! I've just poured water for tea.

AISHA: (nervously) Thank you, Ruth. But you go ahead. I don't want to be making any more trouble for you.

RUTH: You and I both know that tea practically makes itself. Besides, your friend shows up at the door after her husband has been a jerk and we put the kettle on for tea!

AISHA: Oh Ruth, Ali isn't normally a "jerk" as you say. He's usually very sweet.

RUTH: What? Oh, no, I wasn't meaning *Ali*. I meant Roy. Aisha, I'm so, so sorry about Roy and his macho...

AISHA: But it *is* Ali's fault. He provoked Roy who is already suffering from a terrible disease! I'm hoping... we're hoping that you will forgive him.

RUTH: Done and done.

AISHA: He hasn't been himself lately, and then losing his beloved collection of jars, that was a real blow. But I'm not making excuses!

RUTH: Well, we all have trials, don't we? Roy's MS, that's a whopper of a test, but look at you. It can't be easy, being Muslim here. Especially with all the talk about terrorists, and people saying you shouldn't wear your... hijabs, and all.

   RUTH pours the tea.

   There you go. This will make us feel better. (pause) Oh, no, I've done it again. You're still fasting, aren't you? Not even tea?

AISHA: Not for a few days, yet. But thank you.

RUTH: It must be difficult. Here on your own.

AISHA: The mosque is growing, though we do miss the larger Muslim community in Ontario. We had some terrible threats, phone calls, letters, after 9/11. Ali carried much of the burden of feeling he needed to protect us then. And I think it lingers…

RUTH: I can only imagine what that must have been like.

AISHA: We were frightened. Especially when you have children, you want to protect them, you *must* protect them. But most people, especially the people that knew us, were very kind. *(pause)* Like your Jacob.

> *AISHA reaches into her purse, takes out the St. Christopher medal and puts it in RUTH's hand.*

Jacob gave this to Sila, to protect her… it was a kind thing to do. I'm sorry things became confused. Sila is sorry too. She will apologize but she needs just a bit of time to absorb the consequences of her… omission. Ali is sorry too. He needed some time, Allah help him, to climb out of the pit of anger he had dug for himself. And worry. There is worry and fear in that pit as well. The break-in has stirred up a lot.

> *RUTH holds the medal tenderly, running the chain through her fingers.*

RUTH: That pit was crowded, Aisha, with Roy wallowing around in there, too. And I think you're right about the fear. Maybe there's more fear than anger in that pit.

AISHA: Sometimes the fear is first and the anger follows.

RUTH: I thought Roy was going to explode. Ali, too. I'm not sure how we avoided an all-out nuclear melt down.

AISHA: I think a Geiger counter would show some radiation has leaked into the atmosphere, though.

RUTH: To hell with the Geiger counter, what we need here is a giggle counter. There's been too much seriousness! You should really meet my friend at work, Annie. Now there's a lady who knows how to have a good time!

AISHA: Did you just say "to halal" with the Geiger counter? That's the funniest...

RUTH: Did I? I'm the mother of a teenager and the wife of an unhappy, retired postal worker. Anything is possible!

AISHA impulsively reaches out and holds RUTH's hand.

AISHA: Do you think it's possible that we can all be friends? Even after everything that has happened?

RUTH holds the St. Christopher up to the light.

RUTH: But, we already are!

RUTH places her other hand on top of AISHA's.

Look, we both know we can't change our husbands. It's hard enough fighting our own spiritual battles, never mind taking on Muhammad Roy-Ali's, too!

Scene 10

ROY is at home, seated at the kitchen table. He has opened the box of what he thinks are ALI'S jars and he is slowly and methodically taking each one out, turning and inspecting, musing aloud to himself as he does.

ROY: Hebron, Palestinian Territories? Hmm. Could you have been there to fill up your lungs?

ROY carefully places the jar back in the box, and takes the next one out.

ROY: Where you from, fella? Cairo, Egypt? Love, Saskatchewan? *(chuckles)* I do, my dad was born there.

ROY holds the jar up to the light, stares at it in wonder.

You play your cards pretty close to your vest, huh? You and your little glass brothers and sisters. You don't give much away, do you, you rascals?

ROY reaches inside the box. He touches a different jar each time he counts.

ROY: One, two, three … ah, five jars the same.

ROY lines the five jars up on the table.

I wonder if Ali is on to something with all this rarefied air. Maybe these are from Mecca. *(pause)* Or Jerusalem.

A look of hope blooms on ROY's face.

Jesus was crucified there … it's the place of the Resurrection. *(long pause)* Maybe Ali wouldn't mind if I opened just this one? After all, I got them back. And at great expense, at that. It might have healing powers. You never know …

ROY checks the seal on one of the jars, begins to rub the glass carefully over his knees.

JACOB enters the room. VIOLET follows close behind.

JACOB: Whatcha doing Dad?

ROY jumps, startled. He nearly drops the jar.

ROY: What the ... Jesus! *(recovering)* Was crucified there!

JACOB: What?

ROY: What the heck's wrong with you? I just about lost my wig!

VIOLET laughs out loud.

I'm just looking at Mr. Ahmed's collection of jars.

JACOB: I can't believe you made us pay over a hundred dollars to get those back.

VIOLET looks past JACOB's shoulder into the box. She is highly amused by what she sees, a "whoops" expression on her face.

ROY: Thanks to you two big spenders. What were you guys thinking, bidding that high for something that should have gone for a dollar?

JACOB: You're welcome. Mom said to get them back for Mr. Ahmed, so that's what I was going to do.

ROY: What if I'd bid a thousand dollars?

JACOB: *(shrugs)* Mom said to get them back.

ROY: It's been a lesson for all of us.

JACOB: But a good one?

ROY: For you?

JACOB: Yeah, I think so. I kinda got wrapped up in the Islam thing.

ROY: "Thing"?

JACOB: No disrespect. It was more the Sila thing.

ROY: Oh, yeah? Where are you with that?

JACOB: Friends. I think we'll just leave it there.

ROY: Is that good?

JACOB: Yeah.

ROY: We all learned a lesson or two, didn't we? *(pause)* Listen, I'm glad you came in when you did. I was about to let myself open one of Mr. Ahmed's jars. Just to see. I'd tell him, you know.

> *JACOB nods. Long pause.*

JACOB: Sorry, Dad.

ROY: That's okay. I understand, now. I hope Ali…Mr. Ahmed, does, too. About everything, I mean. I gave him a pretty rough going.

JACOB: Muhammad Ali, huh?

ROY: No. I wish I could take that back.

JACOB: You were just sticking up for your kid.

ROY: Yeah.

> *ROY shakes his head.*

No.

JACOB: So are we going to open a jar?

ROY: Should we?

JACOB: Let's do it, Dad. Maybe we'll smell the Holy
          Land. Maybe a genie will come out.

ROY: You wish.

JACOB: Three times.

ROY: There're five jars the same here. Let's try just
          one of them.

> *ROY's eyes light up with excitement as he
> takes a jar off the table. He grasps it in his
> left hand, the lid in his right. As ROY begins
> to turn the lid off of the jar, JACOB comes
> close. Roy breathes in deeply as he opens
> the lid a crack and then again with JACOB
> as the jar is fully open. He stands up beside
> JACOB as he does.*

> *VIOLET breathes, imitating them, from
> the side.*

ROY AND JACOB AND VIOLET: Ahhhhhh.

> *They all breathe out loudly together, then
> ROY sits again, waiting to feel if any change
> has taken place. He moves his arms, his legs,
> checks the palms of his hands, then finally
> looks at JACOB for his reaction. There is a
> long pause. His excitement turns slowly to
> disappointment as the realization comes
> that nothing has changed.*

> *ROY quickly screws the lid back on the jar as
> if it isn't too late to save some of the original
> air from escaping. Both ROY and JACOB look
> sheepish for having allowed themselves to
> get their expectations up.*

> *VIOLET shrugs a what-are-you-going-to-do
> shrug.*

Scene 11

The Gibbons home. VIOLET wanders into the house doing strenuous deep breathing as thought she is giving birth. RUTH is busy at the table preparing food. VIOLET is still puffing away at the edge of the stage, when JACOB walks up. ROY is sitting in a kitchen chair beside a cardboard box. The box is open and there are a couple of jars on the counter and one in ROY's hand that he is examining.

JACOB: *(to RUTH)* What are you making?

VIOLET: I'm making air. Give me a jar to fill. *(still puffing)* Warm air. I can sell it to the popsicle people up north.

RUTH: Something for the Ahmeds.

VIOLET takes an empty jar off the counter and studies it.

JACOB: Oh, not again! You know they can't eat our food. Why would they want to, after what happened.

RUTH: I bought halal chicken from the Persian Place Market. And spices and limes and ginger and garlic and cream...Poor people, hungry all day! They'll need some propping up, some kindness. It'll be a nice added touch to our surprising them with the jars.

JACOB: That should help warm the chill between the Gibbons and the Ahmeds.

VIOLET takes the lid off a jar and begins to take little sips of air from it as if she's tasting wine.

RUTH: Speaking of...Sila's mom was over to say some pretty nice things about you looking out for her daughter. I'm proud of you for that.

JACOB: Really?

> *ROY sits a little more upright in his chair, puts the jar down and turns slightly toward RUTH and JACOB. RUTH wipes her hands with a dish towel, goes into her purse on the counter, takes out the medal and puts it in JACOB's hand.*

RUTH: You might still need this. That's the reason I gave it to you in the first place. It was to look after you.

JACOB: Thanks Mom. I'll keep it safe.

> *ROY rises from his chair and comes up behind RUTH. He wraps his arms around her waist, nuzzles her neck.*

ROY: *(to JACOB)* Isn't your mother amazing? I have no idea how I managed before we met.

RUTH: Let me go right this minute, Roy Gibbons! I have to finish this. Jake, would you separate the cardamom seeds from the pods for your mom?

JACOB: Just as soon as Dad separates himself from you.

ROY: We better listen to your mom, Jake.

JACOB: Seeds and pods? What is this, the Nature Channel?

ROY: *(to RUTH)* Smells good. Are you making enough for all of us, Ruthie?

RUTH: Way ahead of you. Enough for both families. It'll be ready soon.

> *VIOLET exits, smiling with the satisfaction of the pending return to Peace.*

Scene 12

RUTH and ROY are standing outside their home. RUTH is carrying a large casserole dish. She is wearing oven mitts. ROY is juggling a large, awkward box. They walk to the Ahmed home slowly... ROY needs to be careful with his balance.

ROY: Are you okay with that? It's not too hot to carry?

RUTH: I'm fine. Are you?

ROY: Am I what?

RUTH points with her chin to the box ROY is carrying.

Are you okay with that?

RUTH's tone of voice indicates she means more than the box of jars.

ROY: Of course. Heck, I can't wait to see the look on Ali's face when he finds out we've got his jars!

RUTH and ROY arrive at the Ahmeds' door and RUTH manages to ring the doorbell with an oven mittened hand. ALI answers with AISHA behind him.

ALI: Hello!

AISHA: The Gibbons, how nice! Please, come inside.

RUTH: We'd love to, but I've got an early start at work tomorrow.

RUTH holds out the casserole dish.

Please, take this, it's guaranteed halal. Right down to every last cardamom seed!

AISHA and RUTH fumble as RUTH removes the oven mitts and AISHA puts them on, shifting the casserole to AISHA.

AISHA: How lovely! You shouldn't have!

ROY: She can't help it. And it's delicious, by the way. I'm the taste tester.

ROY pauses for a moment, gathering himself.

Ali, there's something else for you … we found your jars!

ROY holds the box out to ALI.

ALI: My … jars?

ROY: Yes, yours.

AISHA: But how?

RUTH: They were at the auction and get this: Roy and Jacob ended up bidding against each other, without knowing it …

ROY: Details, details. The important thing is that you have your jars back. And the air. The air in the jars is all there too …

ALI takes the box of jars. He looks at ROY and RUTH.

ALI: This is incredible! Thank you. This is such a kindness.

AISHA: So thoughtful! Praise be to Allah!

ROY: You'll probably want to set that box down very gently. After all those jars have been through, and not one broken or with any air missing!

ALI and AISHA look puzzled.

RUTH: Well … you want to eat that while it's still warm.

ALI:	Thank you again for this lovely gesture. It helps lighten up the dark corners that those vandals brought into our home, our neighbourhood.
ROY:	Amen to that.

> *RUTH and ROY leave, AISHA and ALI go inside, close the door.*

AISHA:	*(whispers)* Ali, those aren't your jars.
ALI:	Aren't they? *(smiles)*
AISHA:	Yours have labels on them, yes?
ALI:	Yes.

> *AISHA points.*

AISHA:	Those have no labels.
ALI:	Yes.

> *It's AISHA's turn to smile.*

AISHA:	But that's all right now, isn't it?
ALI:	Yes, that's all right.

Scene 13

> *The street outside the Gibbons/Ahmed homes.*

JACOB:	Sila, wait up! I've got a question I want to ask.

> *JACOB jogs to centre stage, where SILA waits for him. He stops a respectable distance away.*

	How are you? I haven't seen you walking to school or back, since, well…for awhile.
SILA:	Oh, hi Jacob. Yeah, Dad's been letting me drive in the mornings. Then he goes on to work from there. *(brightens)* He's reining in

his terror and I'm going to get rid of that "L" sooner rather than later! I'm okay. You?

JACOB: Good! Great, actually. Wow, that hijab makes your eyes pop! Nice colour!

SILA: *(warily)* That's not a question, but thank you, Jacob. What was it you wanted to ask me?

JACOB: I just wanted to know how you were, really? I mean, your parents still aren't upset about the whole St. Christopher thing, I hope?

SILA: They're okay, now. *(pause)* I see you're wearing it again.

JACOB touches St. Christopher medal.

JACOB: Yeah...

SILA: It stopped me from throwing up on the bus, thank God!

JACOB: Praise be to Allah!

Both SILA and JACOB smile.

JACOB: Or maybe you're just growing out of motion sickness. I grew out of my asthma.

SILA: Jacob, I have a question, too.

JACOB: Okay.

SILA: Well... do you think we really would have gone out together, hijab and all? I mean, you asked, but...

JACOB: Yeah, I know what you mean. The hijab is one thing. The "all" part is a whole other thing, right? I mean, Islam is like, your life. Me? I don't even know if I believe in God. Or Allah. Do you know Buddhists don't believe in God?

SILA: Buddhists? So you've moved on from Googling halal and Ramadan, then?

JACOB: But every time my dad talks to yours, he's got a new word he looks up, then he waits for me to come home and I hear all about it.

SILA: Oh dear.

JACOB: No, it's great. Dad's in no shape to throw a football around and it's better than listening to him complain about that tree in your front yard. He hasn't convinced your dad to cut it down yet, has he?

SILA: No, but Dad says he hasn't given up trying!

JACOB: I better get going. Dad's going to take me driving this afternoon. First time. Fingers crossed.

SILA: You'll do great. I'll say a prayer…

JACOB begins to walk away.

JACOB: Bases covered. Maybe we'll see one another out in our cars.

SILA: That would be cool. *(pause)* Aren't you going home?

SILA points in the opposite direction that JACOB is walking.

JACOB: Not yet. I'm meeting Sarah over at her house for a bit.

SILA: Oh.

JACOB: Yeah. Nice to see you, Sila.

SILA: You, too. Bye, Jacob. Safe driving.

Scene 14

ROY and ALI are walking into the Gibbons house. ROY is using his cane again. ALI is carrying a box which he puts down without explanation.

ALI: ...No, I just got to your door. I wasn't waiting any time at all. Besides, it's turned so warm...

ROY: Come on upstairs. You said you wanted to see.

ALI picks up the box again and follows ROY up the stairs.

I was just over helping our new neighbours move in.

ALI: Oh? How are they? *Who* are they? I haven't had the chance yet to meet them.

ROY: The Barbers. They've got a son and daughter. Doug, the father, is a Postie. He's got my old route if you can believe it!

ALI has wandered over to the window. He stands looking down over the neighbour-hood. ROY walks over to join him. ALI looks down at ROY's legs.

ALI: You seem to be getting around pretty well.

ROY: *(laughs)* It's like courage. It comes and goes.

ALI: Yes, I know what you mean.

ROY: It's spring. The saps starts running again in all kinds of things. Even me.

ALI points.

ALI: I see my Chestnut tree has little sons and daughters started all over the place. I've never seen the neighbourhood from up here.

Lights up on VIOLET below.

ALI: Oh, is that one of the new family?

ROY: That's the Barbers' daughter. I think her name is Mollie.

VIOLET waves. ALI is surprised but waves back.

ALI: She's going to think I'm you.

ROY: I don't think there's much chance of that!

ALI: *(a bit puzzled)* She looks familiar. I feel like I've seen her before.

VIOLET smiles.

ALI: She's not much more than Sila's age…

ROY: She'll be at school with my Jacob and your Sila this week. *(pause)* Out with the old…

ROY gestures to himself and ALI.

…and in with beautiful youth…

ROY gives a small wave to VIOLET who again waves back.

ALI: I wonder what it would be like to be that young again?

ROY: I wouldn't know.

Both men laugh. ROY sniffs the air.

ROY: What's that? Is that the smell of regret?

ALI: No. That's the smell of *for*-get.

Both laugh again.

ALI: My wife has a particularly well-developed sense of smell. I thought I had to shower three times a day when we first met. I was afraid of offending her. Then she asked me not to. It turned out she was sensitive to the soap I was using. I used to rejoice when she caught a cold; it was like having a break from responsibility. She knows today what people had for dinner yesterday. She should work for the police. She could smell your son's after-shave when he was half-way home from school. *(pause)* Sorry! I didn't mean to offend.

ROY: No. I threw out that bottle of after-shave he was using weeks ago and I can still smell it. I wrapped it in three bags and, still, it stunk like it was climbing up my arm to do harm to my nose. I would've buried it in the yard but I was afraid it might kill the lawn.

ALI: He's not shaving yet, is he?

ROY: Well … he was. Don't let this get out, but I think he started because of your daughter. Then he was splashing on the smell-good pretty thick. She didn't faint, did she?

ALI: *(laughs)* No.

ROY: Because I nearly did. *(pause)* I've got some coffee made. I don't have a beer in the house. But you don't drink, do you?

ALI: I'd like some coffee. Beer is *haraam*, forbidden.

ROY: By who?

ALI: By Allah.

ROY: *(pause)* Sometimes these things are for our own good. It is forbidden for me, too.

ALI: Yes?

ROY: By my twin. My conscience. Well, not really my twin, I guess. My better half. Not my wife, not *that* better half, but *me.*

ALI: I have a twin. Did you know?

ROY: No.

ALI: No, of course not … My brother. We are not much alike, he and I. He is always calm, never with anger, always patient, a man who can see beyond today to the bigger picture. His name is Shaheer. He sends me jars and makes art.

ROY: An artist?

ALI: He is a farmer who makes art. Is this an artist? I think so. *(pause)* The last time I saw him was at his farm after our mother had died. All the aunts and uncles and cousins were there. All of their children. There were more than sixty of us. It was very nice, but there had been some fighting between some uncles over my mother's last wishes.

Shaheer asked that we go out onto the land and each bring back six stones, even the smallest child did so. He painted each person's stones: some green, some black, then brown, red, blue and white. He laid them out in the sun as if they were scattered there, as though it was random. But at the end of the day he had made a picture, a mosaic there on the ground. It grew and grew...

At this, VIOLET begins to water a small potted pine tree. Beside her is the real box of ALI's jars. When she is finished watering, she begins to open the jars, pouring the air out, freeing it, very pleased with the whole enterprise.

...The mosaic was a picture of our mother sitting under a tree. A fruit tree, her favourite place. He showed us that if you removed even one of those stones, it was as if the picture had shattered. He said it was like peace in a family. *(pause)* My daughter learned that. We learned that, as you know. It is a good thing to learn at least once. *(pause)* I have had to learn it many times.

ROY: Count me in on that long walk.

ALI: "Be good to your neighbours who are strangers, and the friends by your side."

ROY looks to ALI for an answer.

ALI: The Qu'ran.

ROY: Ah. But we are no longer strangers.

ALI: No. Now we are friends. *(pause)* Thank you for returning my jars to me.

> *ALI picks up the box he's brought with him and opens the top flaps. ROY peers inside the box.*

ROY: There's nothing there. What, are you collecting *whole boxes* of air now?

ALI: Again, thank you, but it was best to let it go. I have set it free.

ROY: The air?

ALI: Yes, the jars are just jars, now.

ROY: Empty?

ALI: Yes.

ROY: After all that work getting them back?

ALI: They are happy, freed from their responsibilities as guardians. My wife and daughter are content. I am happy.

> *ROY thinks. He smiles and nods.*

ROY: Then I am, too. *(pause)* Where? Where is the air, now?

> *ALI shrugs.*

ALI: Back with its friends and family. Home. Like you and me.

> *VIOLET continues to open the jars and set the air free as the lights go down.*

— THE END —

Terry Jordan is a Saskatchewan Book award winner and was nominated for the Commonwealth Book Prize. His stage plays have been produced in Canada, the U.S. and Ireland.

Lorna Tureski was born in Hope, British Columbia and spent her early years just past Hell's Gate. Living amongst the Fraser Canyon's intense geography sparked her interest in exploring the fluidity with which one may travel between the practical and the sacred, reconciling the hot-breath intimacy of living and dying. Lorna is a member of the Baha'i community, devoted to the study and practice of what it means to be a world citizen. She has an MFA in Creative Writing from the University of British Columbia and has just completed her first novel.

Arnie Hayashi is on the national board of the Jodo Shinshu Buddhist Temples of Canada. He has spent over twenty-five years working as an advocate of First Nations across Canada and was a key contributor in the design and negotiation of the First Nations Land Management Act. Arnie is a husband, father and grandfather who lives in Vernon with his wife Debra and elderly mother Naoko.